Advance Praise for *Dirty Rotten Strategies*

"*Dirty Rotten Strategies* is insightful, provocative, and important."
—KAREN ARMSTRONG,
best-selling author of *The Spiral Staircase*

"Ian Mitroff has done it again; he and Abraham Silvers have opened our eyes. Here's a lucid and thoughtful account of why we fail to be adequately lucid and thoughtful—and what we can do about it. Bravo!"
—ROBERT B. REICH, Professor of Public Policy, University of California at Berkeley, former U.S. Secretary of Labor, and author of *Supercapitalism: The Transformation of Business, Democracy, and Everyday Life*

"A bracingly powerful book, which should be required reading for all professionals and experts of every stripe. It will liberate all readers from the tyranny of conventional reasoning. The authors give new meaning to Veblen's classic phrase, 'trained incompetence.'"
—WARREN BENNIS, University Professor, University of Southern California, and co-author of *Transparency and Judgment*

"Mitroff and Silvers' amazing book takes away my intellectual, emotional, and spiritual breath—and leaves me virtually without words to capture their startlingly brilliant accomplishment. They offer us a provocative way to rethink the most crucial, bedeviling, complex problems with which we human beings must grapple. They warn us that to do any less is to risk totally annihilating one another as we blithely destroy the planet. If that were not reason enough to read this book, it is also a bona fide page-turner!"
—JEAN LIPMAN-BLUMEN, Thornton F. Bradshaw Professor of Public Policy and Professor of Organizational Behavior, Peter F. Drucker and Masatoshi Ito Graduate School of Management, and author of *The Allure of Toxic Leaders* and *Connective Leadership*

"*Dirty Rotten Strategies* is must reading for everyone. It addresses in ways that are clear, constructive, and often brilliant the undoing of so many well intentioned leaders and administrators—solving the wrong problem precisely. This affliction lies at the heart of many current social problems and this wonderful book offers a way to avoid or lessen it."

—GERALD ZALTMAN, Harvard Business School
and co-author of *Marketing Metaphoria*

"Ian Mitroff and Abraham Silvers nail one of the most pressing challenges of our time. In a deeper way, they show how we can get so distracted by our assessment of a problem that—no matter how well-executed the solution—it can be a complete waste of time, often making the problem much worse! The 'War on Drugs' comes to mind as an example. . . .This book is a wake-up call for problem solvers."

—JOHN RENESCH, futurist and author of
Getting to the Better Future: A Matter of Conscious Choosing

"Mitroff and Silvers suggest that our current challenges are 'wicked problems' that can only be managed by mixing conventional and highly unconventional ways of looking at the world. Incisive and original, *Dirty Rotten Strategies* demonstrates just how valuable systematic thinking can be in helping America to clean up all of its 'messes.'"

—MORLEY WINOGRAD, Executive Director of the Institute
for Communication Technology Management, University of
Southern California Marshall School of Business,
and co-author of *Millennial Makeover*

"Ian Mitroff and Abraham Silvers have written one of the definitive books on the tragedy of well-considered, well-meaning and well-researched error. The great merit of their non-technical, powerful book is the clarity with which they demonstrate that many of the most disastrous decisions are made by brilliantly solving wrongly defined problems. Using a prodigious range of examples from politics, health care, organizational disasters, and national security, they show how cognitive and emotional factors conspire to produce what they term the 'Type Four Error,' in which we mislead not only ourselves but others to act and think in ways directly opposed to generally agreed objectives and values. The book's main contribution is to train us to question the ways we define problems, and to help us avoid some of the errors that we all too easily lapse into. It will be of great value to all those who are perplexed by human ability to repeat mistakes in any field of action and thought."

—YIANNIS GABRIEL, The School of Management, Royal Holloway
University of London, and author of *Organizing Words:*
A Critical Thesaurus for Social and Organization Studies

HIGH RELIABILITY AND CRISIS MANAGEMENT
SERIES EDITORS Karlene H. Roberts and Ian I. Mitroff

SERIES TITLES

High Reliability Management: Operating on the Edge
By Emery Roe and Paul R. Schulman
2008

DIRTY ROTTEN STRATEGIES

*How We Trick Ourselves
and Others into Solving the
Wrong Problems Precisely*

Ian I. Mitroff and
Abraham Silvers

STANFORD BUSINESS BOOKS
An Imprint of Stanford University Press
Stanford, California

Stanford University Press
Stanford, California

Special discounts for bulk quantities of Stanford Business Books are available
to corporations, professional associations, and other organizations. For details
and discount information, contact the special sales department of Stanford
University Press. Tel: (650) 736-1782, Fax: (650) 736-1784

Printed in the United States of America on acid-free, archival-quality paper

Library of Congress Cataloging-in-Publication Data
Mitroff, Ian I.
Dirty rotten strategies : how we trick ourselves and others into solving the
wrong problems precisely / Ian I. Mitroff and Abraham Silvers.
p. cm.
Includes bibliographical references and index.
ISBN 978-0-8047-5996-0 (alk. paper)
1. Problem solving. 2. Errors. 3. Deception. 4. Critical thinking. I. Silvers,
Abraham. II. Title.
BF449.M597 2009
650.1—dc22
2009011622

Typeset by Bruce Lundquist in 10/15 Sabon

This book is dedicated to our children,
Dana Mitroff Silvers and Jonathan Silvers,
and to our newest grandson, Jonah Benjamin Silvers.

If they can get you asking the wrong questions, then they don't have to worry about the answers.

—THOMAS PYNCHON

The worst and most corrupting lies are problems wrongly stated.

—GEORGES BERNANOS

We know . . . that when you cannot get an answer there is something wrong with the question.

—JOAN ROBINSON

CONTENTS

PREFACE

PRÉCIS

Solving the wrong problems precisely is the central topic of *Dirty Rotten Strategies*. If problems are wrongly stated to begin with, then what good are the answers? It is little wonder that we fail repeatedly to make headway on important issues and problems.

Because they are especially fertile sources of errors and because they are so important in their own right, we examine how health care, national security, the media, academia, and religion routinely solve the wrong problems. Even more important, we examine how they routinely foist the wrong problems on us. As a result, we are worse off because what we need are the *right answers* to the *right problems*, and not wasted effort on getting the right answers to the wrong problems. Needless to say, there is no end of other important issues that we could have chosen to examine.

Given that each of these topics reflects our own particular interests, our choices are to a certain extent arbitrary. However, in an important sense our choice of topics is also anything but arbitrary. Health care, national security, the media, academia, and religion are almost guaranteed to appear on anyone's list of major issues. (Although the environment is of paramount importance, and thus is a critical topic in its own right, we discuss it in the context of other issues.)

Although the divisions between the body, mind, and spirit are no longer as clear-cut and sacrosanct as they once were, we examine the health, safety, and security of the body (health care and national security), the mind (the media and academia), and the spirit (religion). The divisions are no longer clear-cut, because any and all of our key problems could be grouped simultaneously under *body, mind,* and *spirit.* The latest evidence from the neurosciences shows how strongly connected, and interconnected, the various aspects of humans are.[1]

In addition, all of our problems are simultaneously political, psychological, philosophical, spiritual, and so on. Therefore, *no single discipline or profession has a monopoly on how we ought to define our key problems.* As a result, the solutions also are not to be found in any single discipline or profession.

AN OPENING EXAMPLE:
ARGUABLY THE BEST IN THE WORLD
American doctors—and more generally, American professionals of any stripe—are arguably the best educated and best trained in the world. Throughout their educations and careers they are exposed to the latest and most advanced technologies. Most important of all, they study under some of the best educators at some of the most prestigious medical schools and research institutes in the world.

Becoming a professional means learning to think and practice in certain highly prescribed ways. Professionals learn to understand and apply highly complex templates, or maps, to complex problems and situations. Both the templates and the problems to which they apply are defined as precisely as possible. Ideally these templates cover the vast majority of problems and situations that the fledging student and beginning practitioner are likely to face—and for the most part they do.

Not only do these templates work but they generally work quite well. Instead of having to remember thousands of separate and disconnected cases and facts, professionals use these maps to reduce the buzzing, booming complexity and confusion of the world—reality itself—down to hundreds of highly stylized situations in as coherent and integrated a manner as possible. The maps make the world comprehensible, and thereby manageable.

In the course of becoming a professional, one learns to think critically, but only within the tight boundaries and narrow confines of accepted thinking within one's chosen field. One does not generally learn to think expansively across different disciplines and different professions. In this sense, one's thinking is also bounded.

Consequently, when one inevitably confronts a problem at the edge, especially a novel problem or a case outside the bounds of accepted thinking, one either is stymied to the point of paralysis or falls back on the only resource one has, thus reducing a novel situation to a problem one already knows how to solve. The trouble is that *the problems one already knows how to solve may bear little resemblance to the problems one actually needs to solve.* As a result, extreme cases and outlier problems and situations pose real and serious challenges to professionals and to the accepted modes of thinking of their professions. In the extreme they lead to serious errors, catastrophic failures, and major disasters and crises.

WHY DOCTORS MAKE SERIOUS ERRORS

We cannot emphasize strongly enough that American doctors are generally acknowledged to be the best trained and best educated doctors in the world. For the most part they perform admirably. Nonetheless, in a highly engaging and important book, *How Doctors Think*, Harvard hematologist Jerome Groopman argues convincingly that, like all professions, the medical profession does not always handle extreme situations and outlier cases very well, because these are precisely the situations that fall outside the generally accepted maps of medical training, research, and practice.[2] Far more frequently than one would like to believe, and certainly far beyond any acceptable standard of adequate care, in dealing with extreme and novel cases, doctors make many bad decisions, serious errors of judgment, and major medical mistakes. As bad as this is, however, it is not the main thrust of Groopman's argument. Much more significant is *why* they make them.

Groopman shows that the vast majority of bad decisions, errors, and mistakes that doctors make are not the result of sheer malice, gross incompetence, or downright stupidity. Instead they are the direct result of the highly standardized ways in which doctors are educated and of the enormous pressures placed on them to think and act quickly and decisively. Although Groopman doesn't use our concepts, it is clear nonetheless that he agrees that the narrowness of medical education—and of professional education in general—and the strains of practice force doctors into *solving the wrong problems precisely.*

Instead of exercising critical thinking, and hence considering multiple options and diagnoses of important issues and problems, doctors are forced by their medical education and by the severe strains of medical practice to use simple checklists and canned diagnostic procedures (algorithms) to treat complex conditions. In other words, checklists and canned procedures substitute for critical thinking. The result is not only the impairment of the health of patients but also, in many cases, serious injuries and even the loss of lives.

THE MORE GENERAL PHENOMENON

Make no mistake about it: Groopman's book is very important. Nonetheless, it is just *one example* of a much more general and troublesome phenomenon. What is true of medicine is true of every profession, but as a result it is truly astounding that the general phenomenon of solving the wrong problems precisely has received virtually no attention or extended discussion.[3] What differentiates this book from others is that solving the wrong problems is its main concern.[4] Indeed, it so important that it deserves its own analysis.

GOING BEYOND

This book goes beyond the individual forms of abuses, crises, and disasters that have overwhelmed us in recent years and that have understandably been overanalyzed, such as the war in Iraq, Enron,

Katrina, and so on. To be sure, it touches on and discusses some of these issues. More important, however, is that it generalizes across each of these individual cases and shows that the problems we face are deep and pervasive.

Just beneath the surface of all the seemingly disparate abuses, crises, and disasters there is a relatively small set of common patterns. By explicitly exposing and analyzing these patterns, we can help to lessen their grip. In short, this book is not a rehash of the books that in recent years have overwhelmed our collective psyche. Instead, it is an analysis of how we define, shape, and make sense of our political and social realities, often to our detriment.

We don't have to accept the narrow and limited definitions of problems that others (single-issue interest groups, big and powerful businesses, academic specialties, and so on) force on us. In other words, there are grounds for hope.

If we couldn't recognize when we were solving the wrong problems precisely, and if there were no ways of assessing when we were doing it, then the situation would truly be hopeless. Furthermore, if we couldn't formulate the concept of solving the wrong problems precisely, then we would have no way of ever knowing what we don't know but desperately need to.

Nonetheless, we would be incredibly naive (which, depending on the topic, all of us are) if we thought that by itself a single book was sufficient to change fundamentally how we formulate, let alone solve, our key problems. All we can hope for is that we have made a good beginning and, as a result, will have stimulated—indeed provoked—others to go beyond where we are.

Whether we have the political and social—and dare we say spiritual?—will and desire to think and act differently is another matter.

ACKNOWLEDGMENTS

No book is ever the product of its authors alone. We owe a debt of gratitude to many people.

First, we thank our families for their untiring and unwavering support. Next, we thank all those with whom we discussed the ideas contained in this book, who read portions of or the entire manuscript and offered invaluable advice: David Brancaccio, Hal Linstone, Judith Rossener, Rob Gunnison, Emery Roe, David Mitroff, and Drexel Sprecher. We would like to thank the following in particular for their comments on Chapter Three: Wesley F. Alles, Jerome V. Blum, Frank R. Ellevitch, Edward P. Richards, and Barbara C. Tilley. We wish we had been wise enough to follow all of their suggestions.

We thank Terry Scott for editing and typing the manuscript, and Stephanie Land for editing parts of an earlier version of Chapter Five. We also thank the anonymous reviewers of both the initial proposal and the final manuscript for challenging our ideas and giving us helpful suggestions.

Finally, we cannot thank enough our editor at Stanford University Press, Margo Beth Crouppen. Margo was a champion of the project from the very beginning. She not only approved the initial idea but also read the entire manuscript and continually offered the finest editorial suggestions we have been fortunate to receive. Whatever errors remain are of our own doing. We hope of course that they are not major examples of solving the wrong problems precisely. We also wish to thank Judith Hibbard, senior production editor at Stanford University Press, and Alice Rowan for their fine editing of the manuscript.

PORTIONS OF CHAPTER FIVE were previously published in Ian I. Mitroff, "Managing Unreality," *Current Topics in Management*, ed. M. Afzalur Rahim, Volume 12, 2007, 89–100. Portions of Chapter Six were previously published in Ian I. Mitroff, "An Open Letter to the Deans and the Faculties of American Business Schools," *Journal of Business Ethics*, Vol. 54, 2004, 185–189; "An Open Letter to the Deans and the Faculties of American Business Schools: A Call to Action," *Academy of Management News*, Vol. 35, No 2, June, 2004, 8–9. Portions of Chapter Seven were previously published in Ian I. Mitroff, "How Do We Know What We Know?" *Journal of Business Strategy*, May/June, Volume 29, No. 3, 2008.

DIRTY ROTTEN
STRATEGIES

1 SCREWING UP ROYALLY

An Introduction to Errors
of the Third and Fourth Kinds

When you have assembled what you call your "facts" in logical order, it
is like an oil lamp you have fashioned, filled and trimmed, but which will
shed no illumination unless first you light it.
—SAINT-EXUPERY, *The Wisdom of the Sands*

It is the nature of an hypothesis, when once a man has conceived it, that it
assimilates every thing to itself as proper nourishment, and, from the first
moment of your begetting it, it generally grows the stronger by every thing
you see, hear, or understand.
—LAURENCE STERNE, *Tristram Shandy*

ERRORS OF THE THIRD KIND

A fundamental concept underlies this entire book: the Error of the
Third Kind.

John Tukey, one of the most famous statisticians ever to have
lived, once said, "Better a poor answer to the right question than a
good answer to the wrong question."[1] Tukey is also reputed to have
said (we paraphrase), "I suspect that most failures occur because we
attempt to solve the wrong problems in the first place, and not because
we fail to get the right solutions to the right problems." Failures occur

because first we get the right solutions to the wrong problems, then we fool ourselves into believing we have solved the right problems to begin with, and finally we stick doggedly to our guns.

Taking Tukey's idea one step further, eminent Harvard decision theorist Howard Raiffa labeled the error of "solving the wrong problem precisely" the Error of the Third Kind, or the Type Three Error (others have worked on the concept of the Type Three Error as well)[2]. Raiffa chose this terminology because Type One and Type Two Errors were already well-established terms within the field of statistics.

As we elaborate on later, the most general definition of the Error of the Third Kind is trying to solve old and new problems with the assumptions, mindsets, and institutions of the past. A Peanuts cartoon from the 1960s says it well. Frustrated by his repeated failures to learn "the new math," Charlie Brown cries out in despair, "How can I learn 'the new math' with an 'old math' mind?" The elementary school teachers who tried to teach the new math were equally frustrated. They too learned painfully that they couldn't teach the new math with an old math mind.

TYPE ONE AND TYPE TWO ERRORS

The basic ideas behind the Type One and Type Two Errors are easy to grasp. Suppose one is interested in testing whether a new drug is better than an old one at treating headaches. In the process of giving the new drug and the old drug to two evenly matched groups (of comparable ages, educations, incomes, jobs, and so on) of, say, a hundred people each (a sample), two errors can be made. First, one can conclude wrongly that the new drug is better than the old one when actually the old one is better or equal to the new one. This is known as the Type One Error, or E1. (In formal statistics, the Type One Error is generally designated as Type I and the Greek symbol α, but for reasons that will become apparent, we're calling it E1 for short.) E1 is akin to saying that there is a meaningful difference between the two drugs when there is not. Second, one can also conclude wrongly that the old drug is better than the new one when in fact the new one is better. This is known as the Type Two Error, or E2. [3] E2 is akin to saying that there is *not* a meaningful difference between the drugs when there is.

There is a natural variance in how people react to particular drugs. Depending on the circumstances, some people react more strongly than others. (Think of the familiar bell-shaped curve.) The results from the tests can therefore be misleading and hence lead to false conclusions.

For instance, suppose that, purely by chance, on a particular day a majority of the people taking the new drug are unusually re-sponsive to it and a majority taking the old drug are unusually *un*-responsive to it. We would then conclude, purely by chance, that the new drug is better than the old one when it may not be better at all. (This might happen, for example, if we pull an unrepresenta-tive sample of people from the *upper* end of the bell-shaped curve to test the new drug and an unrepresentative sample of people from the *lower* end of the same bell-shaped curve to test the old drug.) If on other days we use other groups to compare the drugs, we might get completely different results.

Statisticians design testing procedures that attempt to control for both kinds of errors. Because it is generally impossible to minimize both errors simultaneously—one error typically increases as the other decreases—one has to choose which error is more important to minimize in a particular situation. For instance, it may be more important to keep using a trusted and tried drug in which one has high confidence than to replace it with a new one that has potentially serious and unknown side effects, such as Vioxx. Thus, it may be more important to say that the old drug is better than the new one in terms of controlling for side effects, whereas the new one is actu-ally better in treating some conditions. In other words, in this case it may be prudent to be conservative and to side with the old drug until it is conclusively proven to be inferior. One is thus willing to tolerate larger Type Two Errors than Type One Errors. (Remember, we commit a Type One Error if we conclude wrongly that the new drug is better than the old one when in fact the old one is better.

Conversely, we commit a Type Two error if we conclude wrongly that that the old drug is better than the new one when actually the new one is better.)

Although the Type One and Type Two Errors are taught in virtually every course in statistics, no matter how elementary or advanced, the Type Three Error is almost never discussed. The reason is that the Type One and Type Two Errors involve only a technical knowledge of statistics, while in contrast the Type Three Error demands wisdom—the ability to be aware of and rise above our biases and passions. In short, it requires the ability to exercise critical thinking, to be aware of and challenge our basic assumptions. Even though critical thinking is supposed to be the fundamental purpose of education, it is rarely taught, let alone in statistics. In this sense, the Type Three Error is not only beyond the field of statistics, it also comes prior to it. Indeed, it is prior to every field of knowledge.

Another way to put it is to say that managers and technicians focus on Type One and Type Two Errors, and leaders focus on Type Three Errors. Famed management consultant and theorist Peter Drucker put it as follows: "Managers and technicians do known things right; leaders ask what are the right things to do."

If the Type One and Type Two Errors hadn't already been invented, it is clear that Raiffa would have labeled the Error of the Third Kind the Type One Error, or even more fundamental, The Type Zero Error. The choice is more than one of terminology alone. Calling the Type Three Error the Type One, or Type Zero, Error would have made it perfectly clear not only that Errors of the Third Kind *come before* Type One and Type Two Errors, but also that Errors of the Third Kind are *more fundamental*. After all, Type One and Type Two Errors can be determined only *after* one has already defined the problem.

Raiffa's whole point was this: What good does it do to minimize or control for Type One and Type Two Errors if the problem one is attempting to solve is wrong to begin with? This is precisely the question that good leaders ask.

For instance, instead of posing the problem as one of determining whether a new drug is more efficacious than an old one in relieving pain, suppose the problem is how to develop a cheaper, generic version of the old drug. Of course ideally one would like to do both, that is, produce a generic version of a new drug that is *both more effective and cheaper* than the old one. Because in principle the two problems are not exactly the same, the Type Three Error forces us to ask, and thereby to decide, which is more important to obtain: a newer and more effective drug, or a cheaper version of an old one.

Even more basic, the Type Three Error, or E3, forces us to ask whether the problem is not one of taking a cheaper or better drug but rather one of making changes in lifestyle and diet.

ERRORS OF THE FOURTH KIND

As important as the Type Three Error is, we believe that a far more serious and potentially dangerous type of error needs to be addressed. This is the Error of the Fourth Kind, or the Type Four Error.

The Type Three Error is the unintentional *error of solving the wrong problems precisely. In sharp contrast, the Type Four Error is the* intentional *error of solving the wrong problems.* Although Tukey and Raiffa clearly foresaw the Type Three Error—they literally invented it—they did not clearly distinguish between Type Three and Type Four Errors. In other words, they conflated both errors. In this sense, they did not foresee the Type Four Error. Although the two types are often connected (Type Four Errors are often the direct result of Type Three Errors), they are not exactly the same; thus they need to be distinguished from each other.

The Type Three Error is primarily the result of ignorance, a narrow and faulty education, and unreflective practice. In contrast, the Type Four Error is the result of deliberate malice, narrow ideology, overzealousness, a sense of self-righteousness, and wrongdoing. As we shall see repeatedly, every Type Four Error is invariably political or has strong political elements, in both the broad and narrow senses of the term; but then so do the Type One and Type Two Errors, even if their political elements are more hidden and therefore more difficult to see. For example, saying that a Type One Error is more important than a Type Two Error is often the result of political decisions or elements. It certainly is affected by organizational politics.

The Type Three Error occurs when to *our* detriment *we* un-*intentionally fool and trick ourselves* into solving the wrong problems precisely, *but we don't necessarily force our definitions on others.* In sharp contrast, the Type Four Error occurs when, to *their* detriment and for *our* gain and benefit, *we intentionally force others* into solving the wrong problems precisely. That is, in the Type Four Error we force and trick others into solving *our* definitions of problems.

In brief, we *unintentionally* mislead *ourselves* when we commit a Type Three Error, whereas we *intentionally* mislead *others* when we commit a Type Four Error, or E4.

Notice that there are no absolutely certain, precise, or fixed differences between E3 and E4. It is a natural tendency to want to convince others that the problems we are working on are the correct ones. In this sense, every E3 has within it the potential to become an E4. The differences between E3 and E4 are thus matters of degree, not of kind.

It would seem logical that once one has committed an E4, it is then impossible to commit an E3 in regard to the same problem. In other words, it would seem that the arrow of causality goes from E3 to E4, but not from E4 to E3. Once one has *intentionally forced* on others the wrong definition of a problem, it is then impossible to claim that one has *un*intentionally solved the wrong problem. The trouble with this line of reasoning is that people and organizations do not reason according to the dictates of pure logic. People and organizations are perfectly capable of believing and doing the most outlandish and outrageous things. Another way to put it is to say that people and organizations are perfectly capable of switching back and forth, or sliding, from intentional to unintentional states of belief, actions, and so on, and vice versa, often without full or conscious awareness.

The upshot is that a single person, organization, or society cannot by itself determine whether it is committing an E3 or an E4. The nature of the error must be determined by *at least one* other person or organization that does not share the same belief system as the person, organization, or society that is committing the error.

The differences between E3 and E4 are most pronounced and therefore most easily observed when accepting a particular definition of a problem has important consequences for large numbers of people. Although all of us will make many Type Three Errors over the course of our lives, not all of them will rise to the level of Type Four. (One could of course argue that voting is the major means by which the average citizen has the opportunity to commit E4s.)

Finally, as the following examples show, both individuals and organizations (and certainly whole societies) are capable of committing E3 and E4. Neither error is the sole or exclusive province of one or the other.

A CASE STUDY OF THE FAILURE TO THINK
CRITICALLY: THE BELGIUM COCA-COLA CRISIS

In mid-1999, after a huge outcry of negative public opinion and the adverse decision of the health minister of Belgium, Coca-Cola was forced to recall about thirty million cans and bottles of its products (Coke, Fanta, and so on).[4] Not only was this the largest product recall in the company's 113-year history, but for the first time ever the entire inventory of Coca-Cola products was banned from sale throughout Belgium.

The ways in which Coca-Cola mishandled the Belgian crisis was not only one of the worst public relations disasters in the company's history, but also one of the biggest textbook examples of how *not* to do crisis management. The crisis resulted not only in the loss of millions of dollars for the company, but also in the eventual firing of Coca-Cola's CEO, Ken Ivester. Like most crises, the story has a number of elements, or subplots, most of which are examples of E3 and E4.

The crisis began when children at six schools in Belgium complained that the Coke products they had consumed tasted and smelled funny. Soon afterward they suffered serious headaches, nausea, vomiting, and shivering. The symptoms ultimately led to their being hospitalized. The same week, the governments of France, the

Netherlands, and Luxembourg also banned Coca-Cola's products. The company's Dutch arm recalled all products from its Belgium plant, and 240 Belgian and French citizens, mostly school children, were left ill after drinking Coke products produced at the Antwerp and Dunkirk facilities. How Coca-Cola responded to the crisis revealed not only how deeply flawed its understanding of crisis management was but also how easily and quickly it became trapped in solving the wrong problem precisely. The first response of the company's top executives was to have their quality control engineers run extensive tests on the products in question. The engineers quickly ascertained that there was nothing toxic in the beverages; therefore, from a health standpoint, there was nothing wrong with the products. They tasted and smelled funny only because of the substandard carbon dioxide that was used to carbonate them. As far as it went, this part of Coca-Cola's strategy was OK. They had not yet committed an error of solving the wrong problem precisely.

With this explanation in hand, Coca-Cola's executives thought, naively, that the crisis was over and hence would quickly go away. Given a "rational explanation" for the funny smell and taste of the beverages, the children, their families, and the Belgian health minister would see the products as acceptable, and the ban against them would be lifted. The trouble with this "solution" was that it made things worse, not better. It not only exacerbated the initial crisis but set off a chain reaction of new crises as well.

The executives who were involved in handling the crisis said not only that there was nothing wrong with their beverages but also that the reactions of the children, their families, and the Belgian health minister were due to mass hysteria, that their reactions were merely psychological and therefore should be dismissed out of hand. In this way, Coca-Cola's executives not only attempted to explain the problem away, but also did something far worse. They basically insulted their consumers, their families, and the health minister of Belgium. As a result, not only did sales plummet throughout Europe, but MacDonald's, one of Coca-Cola's largest and most important customers, stopped selling Coke in all of its European fast food outlets.

In accepting the definition of the problem as primarily technical, that is, as a problem of quality control and quality assurance, not only were Coca-Cola's executives solving the wrong problem precisely, but they were also violating one of the cardinal rules of crisis management: never, ever insult your customers or key stakeholders, especially children and their parents. Instead, always go out of your way to demonstrate empathy and to convey honest compassion and sincere concern for them.

Without knowing it, Coca-Cola's executives were trapped by a number of forces, many of their own making: a strong corporate culture that reinforced a group mentality (groupthink), the narrowness and similarity of their professional backgrounds and education, their overwhelming concern with profits, and the intense fears associated with the fact that Coke sales had been steadily declining worldwide. All of these factors predisposed them to think alike and hence to define the problem—the crisis—as primarily and inherently technical. Ironically, even though, when it came to advertising, marketing, and sales, outside psychologists and marketing consultants as well as in-house staff played a big role (Coca-Cola's ads and marketing campaigns were regularly touted as among the best in the industry), psychologists or other social scientists were not part of the team when it came to handling major crises.

Other ways of looking at how Coca-Cola defined the problem bring out additional features of the crisis. In responding to the Belgium situation, the company's top executives considered their quality control engineers to be the primary and relevant experts. Indeed, from their perspective, the engineers were the *only* relevant experts and the primary stakeholders. In contrast, the Belgian health minister and the families of the children considered the children to be the primary and relevant experts. The experts were different in each case because each side defined—that is, felt and experienced—the problem differently.

In other words, the Coca-Cola's top executives assumed implicitly that everyone was a quality control engineer, and in contrast the Belgian health minister assumed implicitly that everyone was a government-appointed official concerned primarily with keeping his or her job. How wrong they both were! Nonetheless, Coca-Cola's executives were "more wrong."

What's sad is that in a fundamental sense both definitions of the crisis or problem are correct. As a matter of fact, each is fundamentally incomplete without the other. Like essentially all problems in a complex world, the Coke crisis was not an either-or but a both-and problem. The complete or true definition of the problem was both psychological and technical. In this sense, Coca-Cola's executives were solving only part of the problem. *They were solving the wrong problem because they were not solving the total problem.* The problem was not primarily how to ensure the quality of its products but how to assuage the fears of its primary customers.

But the Belgian health minister was not solving the full problem either. In this sense, he was committing both an E3 and an E4. However, he didn't need to solve the complete problem, because he was responding to and representing the offended parties against an uncaring and unfeeling corporate bully.

Like most executives, Coca-Cola's made a number of unstated and faulty assumptions. First, if the problem was literally not in the Coke, then there was not a real problem. Second, conversely, the problem with or in the children was not real. Third, the reactions of the children could be explained away as mass hysteria. Fourth, and most basic of all, psychological problems are not as important, or as real, as physical ones.

In the end, we rise and we fall by the basic assumptions we make about others, the world, and ourselves. As we shall see, in every case, solving the wrong problem precisely can be traced to a set of faulty, largely unstated, and unconscious assumptions.

The Source and Nature of Coca-Cola's Error
One of the most common and most prevalent reasons that an individual, an organization, or even a whole society commits the error of solving the wrong problem is a narrow belief system. In turn, a narrow belief system is often the product or reflection of a narrow

political ideology or company culture, of a limited philosophical worldview, education, family background, and so on. Whatever the source, a narrow belief system generally leads to a single definition of a problem, a definition that is accepted beyond question and hence staunchly defended.

This is not, however, the only cause of committing the error of solving the wrong problem. Fear, psychological frame of mind, and personality also play important roles. In addition, the inability to exhibit genuine empathy for others is an important factor. Narrowness and strong similarities in educational and professional backgrounds are sufficient in most cases to account for why most people and most groups quickly zero in on a single, preferred, and "natural" definition of a problem. Groupthink is an important mechanism for producing the error of solving the wrong problem precisely.

But what accounts for lack of empathy and remorse for others? Unfortunately, there is growing evidence that those who rise to high positions of authority and power are in far too many cases what are termed *avoidant personalities.*[5] Avoidants typically do not consider the feelings of others, because they have little need for other people. As a result, they are extremely comfortable ignoring others' feelings.[6] That is, they exhibit little or no visible feeling of anxiety when ignoring others. They also exhibit little remorse or guilt in using others to their advantage. (The executives and energy traders of Enron are a classic example of this.)

Now, of course we have no way of knowing for sure whether these factors were operating in the case of Coca-Cola's executives, but we do know from all of our consulting opportunities over the years that in both the so-called public and private sectors these factors are present in far too many situations, for we have observed them firsthand. We are therefore strongly inclined to bet that they were major operating factors in the Belgium Coke crisis as well. Furthermore, the psychological literature says that in times of extreme stress—which is present in essentially all crisis situations—one's default way of coping with stress comes to the fore.[7] The psychological literature also says that a person's characteristic way of responding to and coping with stress is learned from one's primary caretakers, beginning at birth.[8] How a person's parents respond to stress is one of the strongest factors in how that person responds to stress. This means that unless one is aware of it and seeks active intervention, one cannot break and change the pattern. It is little wonder, then, that the error of solving the wrong problem precisely is committed so often. Indeed, what requires explanation is why we don't have more such errors.

Actually, like very small earthquakes, such errors occur all the time. However, most of them occur beneath the threshold of the public's and the media's attention. This has the effect of lulling us into complacency so that when a really big one hits (such as the credit crisis), we are generally unprepared to deal with it effectively.

Coca-Cola clearly committed a Type Three Error in Belgium, and throughout Europe. We believe they also committed a Type Four Error, even though they were spectacularly unsuccessful in getting the parents and the Belgian health minister to accept their definition of the problem. Their intention to get others to accept their flawed definition was the critical factor that moved them from committing a Type Three Error to committing a Type Four Error.

The Aftermath

One of the many Web sites devoted to an analysis of the Coke crisis summed up the financial consequences as follows:

Coca-Cola's financial performance suffered a major setback due to the Belgian crisis. The recall had a negative impact on Coca-Cola's overall second-quarter net income in the fiscal year 1999, coming down by 21% to $942 million. Moreover, the entire operation of removing and destroying recalled products cost Coca-Cola Enterprises $103 million (£66 million) in 1999 dollars. The recall led to a 5% decline in the bottler's revenues and a fall in cash operating profit by 6%. Coca-Cola's brand image was hit among Belgian consumers; a market that had been one of Europe's most successful for the company.[9]

Crises have the potential to cost big. How we respond to them has the potential to make them cost even more.

ANOTHER EXAMPLE OF SOLVING
THE WRONG PROBLEM PRECISELY: PCBS

Several years ago, Abraham Silvers had the opportunity to work for the Electric Power Institute as a research statistician. Although there was not yet an airtight case, strong evidence had already accumulated to the effect that not only were polychlorinated biphenyls (PCBs) seeping into the environment, but they were posing a serious danger to human health.

At an important meeting of companies in industry, a senior science consultant on the staff of a large utility said publicly that he thought PCBs had to be controlled in order to protect the health of workers and of citizens in nearby communities. He argued that the industry ought to get out in front of the issue and do everything in its power to take responsible action to control its use of PCBs. (Interestingly enough, he was later to become the expert toxicologist for Erin Brockovich in her suit against the giant utility PG&E.)

As soon as the consultant made this statement, someone from another company blurted out, "Right here in front of me, I have a cup filled with PCBs. I am willing to drink it right now to prove that it is not a threat to human health!" Obviously he had prepared well in advance of the meeting. (He might have been correct in the short run, because the danger to his health probably would not have shown up for years.)

Now, we can't know for sure whether he actually would have drunk the foul stuff or whether he was just bluffing and going for theatrics. The point is that he was willing to commit not only a Type Four Error on others but also a Type Three Error directly on himself! Of course *he* didn't see it that way at all. *He* didn't see himself as committing an error. Instead, he saw *others* as the ones who were making a huge error.

If the problem was how to attract maximum attention to his position by doing something overly dramatic, then he was indeed solving the right problem; but if the problem was how to avoid potentially toxic substances entering the animal and human food chain, and to exercise caution in protecting and serving the greater public good, then he was indeed solving the wrong one.

Naturally the person who volunteered to drink the cup of PCBs was later found to have been supremely wrong, even if he was unable to admit it. As the following example shows, dumb acts and dumb arguments are almost always a fundamental part of all errors of solving the wrong problem precisely.

DON IMUS:
A CASE OF HIGHLY FLAWED ASSUMPTIONS

Recall the case of radio and TV personality Don Imus, who was fired in 2007 for using racially insensitive and slanderous terms to describe the members of the Rutgers University women's basketball team. (He was subsequently hired by another network.) Although we don't know for sure, we bet that prior to Imus's firing, he and his producers assumed something like the following:

1. By virtue of his or her unique occupation and position in society, a comic has a special license (social contract) to attack almost anyone or anything without serious retribution or payback. As part of this special social contract, a comic also has the license to use racially insensitive and vitriolic language. In other words, comics are generally immune and shielded from censure and criticism. (Go tell this one to comedian Michael Richards of *Seinfeld*, who used a racial epithet against black members of the audience who were heckling him at one of his performances, thereby virtually ending his career.)

2. Whenever the members of a particular group (in this case, African Americans) use demeaning language, such as a highly offensive epithet (in this case, "nappy-headed hos"), against the other members of their very own group, then I am warranted in using it as well. In short, the assumption is, if they can do it, I can as well.

3. The fact that I have gotten away with outrageous, over-the-top behavior for more than thirty years guarantees that I can get away with it one more time, if not indefinitely. (Notice that not only is this a continuity assumption—the future will be like the past—but the larger the number of times one has gotten away with something in the past, then the greater the guarantee that one will get away with it one more time.)

4. Outrageous behavior sells. One has to be continually edgy in order to attract and keep mass audiences. One has to always push the envelope.

5. If I don't push the boundaries, then someone else will. Hence I'm forced to do it. I have no other choice. It's a dog-eat-dog business.

6. Attacking or making fun of young women is in principle no different from attacking adults who willingly come on to my show to hawk themselves, their celebrity, their books, their political candidacies, and so on. In short, anyone in the public eye is fair game for attack and ridicule.

7. The fact that I contribute large sums of money to worthy causes for extremely deserving children further insulates me from attack.

Although these assumptions—and by calling them assumptions we are being far too kind—may have been true for a long time, Imus's case shows how quickly and completely assumptions can collapse. In short, on the basis of the preceding assumptions, Imus and his producers successfully solved the problem of how to attract and hold a large radio audience for a long time. What they did not solve was what to do if and when their assumptions were no longer valid.

Once again, if there is a single underlying reason that we solve the wrong problems precisely, it is that we are prisoners of a set of assumptions that are deeply flawed, out-of-date, or just plain wrong. We are the prisoners of our assumptions because, more often than not, we don't even know what our assumptions are, and we don't know that we are making all kinds of assumptions about others, the world, and ourselves. In short, we are unconscious of our basic assumptions.

THREE EXAMPLES

The three cases of Type Three and Type Four Errors that we have considered in this chapter—Coke, PCBs, and Don Imus—are merely three examples of a more general phenomenon. In the rest of this book we look at many more examples drawn from academia, business, government, the media, and religion. In this way we show how widespread the phenomenon is, as well as general strategies for breaking ourselves free from these most problematic errors.

For example, in Chapter Three we discuss how a Type Four Error occurs when the medical system does everything in its power to convince us that health care is just a product that can be bought and sold like any other product, and that the primary objective of the system is controlling costs and not promoting our general health and well-being. It solves the problem of controlling costs by getting others to bear them. It does not solve the fundamental problem of promoting our general health and well-being. A Type Four Error occurs when even those who have medical insurance are denied coverage because to do so makes the system even more profitable. The medical insurance system has a huge incentive to reward handsomely those claims agents and adjustors who are very good at finding ways to deny insurance claims, coverage, and payments. In other words, the system solves quite well the problem of how to deny coverage to those who have paid for it and deserve it—but this is not a problem worth solving, let alone solving well.

A Type Four Error also occurs when the big HMOs and medical insurance companies do everything in their power to convince us that they are justified in making huge profits at our expense. As such, the real business they are in is that of convincing us that the way they define the problem of health care is the true definition of the problem. From their standpoint, the primary problem is holding down costs, not helping us get and stay healthy. Thus, a broad problem—how to get and stay healthy—is converted into a narrow problem (although one that is important nonetheless).

The book by Jerome Groopman to which we referred in the Preface is primarily about how, when, and why individual doctors are likely to commit Type Three Errors.[10] It is not about Type Four Errors, which arise mainly from the medical system as a whole, and in particular from the dirty tricks and other dirty rotten strategies of the big insurance and drug companies.

To put all of this in perspective, the medical system commits a combination of Type One and Type Two Errors when it says it delivers high-quality care at an affordable price when in fact it does not. In contrast, it commits a Type Four Error when it does everything in its power to convince us that the private enterprise system is the best and only way to solve the problems of health care. In other words, a Type Four Error occurs when the medical system defines the problems of health care mainly on the basis of its own political and philosophical ideology.

A Type Four Error also occurs when big businesses and major corporations use criminal and deceitful tactics to make obscene profits at the expense of the public's health, safety, and well-being. A Type Four Error especially occurs when they try to convince us not only that all of this is acceptable in the name of capitalism, but also that this is the "natural order of things," that is, that the system is as it should be. For instance, the error occurs when CEOs try to convince us that they are justified in making astronomical amounts of money in comparison to the lowest-paid persons in their organizations. CEOs have learned quite well how to solve the problem of how to earn outrageous sums of money at the literal expense of other people in their organizations.

One of the biggest Type Four Errors of all occurs when we put our enormous energies into developing a virulent form of capitalism that Robert Reich has called *supercapitalism* and Naomi Klein has called *disaster capitalism*.[11] Although there is much in Reich's and Klein's work with which we agree, and as bad as they make contemporary capitalism out to be, we think it is far worse than they have described. On the one hand, *supercapitalism* is too mild a term; on the other hand, although it is much stronger than Reich's term, *disaster capitalism* is not strong enough. We prefer to call contemporary capitalism *sociopathic capitalism*. By this we mean that modern capitalism has a number of the critical characteristics associated with sociopathology, for example, the commission of unethical acts intentionally designed to hoodwink the public; the glorification of unethical behavior, such as unrestrained greed; and little or no guilt associated with deceptive and unethical behavior. Clearly Enron and other major organizations that have been convicted of wrongdoing more than fit the bill.[12]

So do the mortgage companies that tricked people into taking out loans that they had no ability, or intention, to repay. The people who took out such loans are guilty as well. As with most crises, there is more than enough blame to go around. Thus the government regulators who failed to do their job are also at fault; and by failing to pass tougher rules and regulations, Congress must share a large part of the blame. In short, as a society we have solved the wrong problem, that is, how to create an especially virulent and dangerous form of capitalism—sociopathic capitalism.

A Type Four Error also occurs when government uses disinformation and misinformation to get us to accept ill-conceived and disastrous policies that trample on civil rights, privatize social security, mistreat gays, and send the children of the poor to die in illegitimate and poorly conceived wars. A Type Four Error occurs when the legislative branch of government fails to exercise its checks and balances on the executive in order to, for example, provide proper oversight on the conduct of the Iraq war. That is, a Type Four Error occurs when the legislative branch does not solve the problem of how to provide effective oversight. A Type Four Error occurs when instead of curbing terrorism, the war in Iraq actually furthers and strengthens it.

As we show later, one of the most prevalent forms of the Type Four Error occurs when we assume wrongly that increasing without limit something (such as actions or means) that is good in small quantities always leads to good outcomes (ends). Beyond a certain point, more does not lead to more; instead, it turns back on itself so that more leads to less. For example, in fighting conventional wars, larger armies are generally superior to smaller ones; but in fighting unconventional wars, bigger is not always better, let alone best.

A Type Four Error occurs when the media knowingly and willingly go along with illicit government policies, when they abdicate their role as critics and checks on the abuses and powers of government. Although many journalists (mainly print) were of course critical of the Iraq war from the very beginning, the system as a whole failed to do its job. Indeed, the Iraq war is a case study in the failure of almost every system that was supposed to protect us from such follies.

A Type Four Error occurs when the media invent and use the cleverest and most technologically sophisticated forms of unreality that not only distract us but actually diminish our ability to deal with ever-growing, complex forms of reality. Unreality not only makes the unreal look as real as reality, but it also makes it look better than and thus preferable to reality. The result is that not only is it increasingly difficult to distinguish between what's real and what's not—between what's true and what's false—but we no longer care to distinguish between them, assuming that we still could.

A Type Four Error occurs when the media feed, nurture, and intensify the public's insatiable need for pseudo celebrities, and then turn around and argue that they are just fulfilling a pent-up, already existing and natural demand, not creating an artificial one. The truth is that the media both create new needs and wants and meet and fuel old ones.

A Type Four Error occurs when our colleges and universities abdicate their primary role of teaching us how to think critically, that is, when they do not teach us about Type Three and Type Four Errors and how to lower our chances of committing them. Such errors occur especially as the result of carving up the world into disciplines that are no longer suited to the problems we face. In other words, colleges and universities are largely wedded to an outmoded, largely nineteenth-century solution for the organization of knowledge.

A Type Four Error occurs when special-interest groups over-emphasize the uncertainties in scientific research on, for example, global warming and thereby deliberately distort and downplay the widespread agreement that exists in the scientific community.

Karen Armstrong has pointed out masterfully that the major religions of the world are the products of a long-gone Axial Age.[13] They are the "solutions" to the economic, social, and spiritual problems of five thousand years. They no longer work as complete solutions to today's problems. Instead of continuing to solve the problems of a bygone age, and hence committing Type Three and Type Four Errors in the name of religion, we need new conceptions of God that are better suited to the problems of our times.

CAN WE EVER KNOW FOR SURE?

Can we ever know for sure that we are solving the wrong problems? How can we determine that others are attempting to force us into solving the wrong problems precisely? These are just two of the important questions that we address in this book.

The short answer is that we can never know for sure that we are committing a Type Three Error, but there are nearly always strong indicators and signals that we are about to commit one. Although they are not perfect, there are ways of assessing whether we or others are committing Type Three and Type Four Errors, and there are ways of avoiding them. Nonetheless, we do not assume that even if we could detect such errors everyone is equally concerned with avoiding them.

Before we end this chapter, we explore the concepts of the Type Three and Type Four Errors a bit more by means of an instructive joke.

A DEATH-DEFYING LOGIC

A man walks into a psychiatrist's office.

The psychiatrist asks, "What's your problem?"

The man says, "I'm convinced that I'm dead, but I'm having trouble persuading anyone else."

The psychiatrist says, "OK," and agrees to work with the man.

After six months, the psychiatrist turns to the man in frustration and asks, "Look, if I can prove to you that you're not dead, will you give up the belief that you are?"

The man says, "Of course!"

"Well, you don't believe that dead men bleed, do you?"

"No, of course not; that's impossible!"

With that, the psychiatrist takes out a small pin from his desk drawer, reaches over, and pricks the man so that a tiny drop of blood appears on his arm.

The man looks down at the blood and exclaims,

"Why, I'll be damned! Dead men do bleed!"

Humans are truly amazing creatures. They have an incredible ability to fabricate and shape reality to suit their needs. If someone is deeply committed to an assumption or a belief, then all of the evidence and arguments to the contrary are often of little use in causing the person to abandon them. Jonathan Swift put it best of all: "It is useless to attempt to reason a man out of a thing he was never reasoned into."

As the joke demonstrates, evidence and arguments to the contrary—such as deliberately showing a person that he can bleed—can even cause a person to hold his or her beliefs more strongly. (Witness President Bush and how he reacted to the "fact" that the intelligence agencies confirmed that for the past few years Iran was not developing a nuclear weapons program.) Evidence and arguments that are disconfirming for others are confirming for the person who holds a particular belief.

We especially resist that which threatens our basic sense of who and what we are. Thus, in the joke just presented, in order for the man to give up the belief that he is dead he would have to know the fundamental purposes it serves. In brief, what is he getting out of it? If he believes that he is already dead, then perhaps he also believes that he can never die—in short, that he is immortal. Does his belief thereby allow him to evade normal human responsibilities such as walking the dog and taking out the trash?

Humans have believed even stranger and wilder things than this, and we should not automatically rule them out just because they may seem odd, if not crazy, to us. But there are even deeper reasons that we often resist the truth. Take the case of Galileo. Is anyone really naive enough to believe that the Church Fathers should have *immediately* given up fifteen hundred years or so of sacred dogma just because someone claimed to have observed something strange and wonderful through a small metal tube with two pieces of glass at either end? What's a small metal tube compared to the majesty of Church dogma that by definition cannot be "directly observed" by the naked eye? One sees sacred objects with the soul, not with the senses.

We say this having doctorates—Ian Mitroff's in engineering science with a minor in the philosophy of social science, and Silvers' in pure mathematics. Both of us therefore believe deeply in rationality and science, but we also believe in psychology and philosophy. Even though we generally do not side with the Church in matters of belief, we can nonetheless see the Church's point in the case of Galileo. The Church was not wrong to resist, *in the beginning.*

Although it is unreasonable to expect anyone to give up his or her cherished assumptions and beliefs immediately,[14] it is not unreasonable to expect a person to give them up after "sufficient evidence" to the contrary has accumulated. If we were required to give up our assumptions and beliefs at the first signs of disconfirmation and doubt, then we would be forced to give up virtually all of our assumptions and all of our beliefs all of the time. Such a world is completely untenable. There would be little if any continuity. No one could function in it.

To a degree, but only to a degree, hanging onto our basic assumptions and beliefs is rational;[15] but when evidence to the contrary has not only accumulated but is overwhelmingly against our basic beliefs and assumptions, then hanging onto them is not only irrational but a sign that something is seriously wrong in ourselves and our body politic.

For instance, the following example from the field of national politics is as dangerously close to Dead Men Do Bleed as one could ever hope to find:

> [Karl] Rove [President Bush's chief political advisor] suggested, as Bush repeatedly has, that history will ratify the decision to invade Iraq. "You know, the Bush doctrine—'Feed a terrorist, arm a terrorist, train a terrorist, fund a terrorist, you're just as bad as a terrorist,'" he said. "It's going to remain our national doctrine, and it's going to be very difficult, I think, if not impossible, to dismiss this, just as it will be to dismiss the doctrine of preemption. In the future, the country is not going to let the dangers fully materialize, and we're not going to allow ourselves to be attacked before we do anything about it. The question was, did we have the right intelligence about Saddam Hussein? No. Was it the *right* thing to do? Yes."[16]

Even after they are long gone from the public stage, what, if anything, could possibly disconfirm and thus cause President Bush and Karl Rove to abandon their belief that the invasion of Iraq was "right"? Apparently, nothing. Dead men do bleed after all. (We cannot emphasize too much that even when it was revealed that Iran had not been pursuing a nuclear weapons program as the administration had repeatedly contended, this served only to strengthen President Bush's belief that Iran might develop one someday.)

The point of the preceding example is not to call attention to whether or not the reader shares our political beliefs—our biases, if you will—but to show once again that fundamental differences in views are required to determine whether an E3 or an E4 is being committed. In other words, the views of those who are determining whether an E3 or E4 error has been committed must obviously be different from the views of those who are committing the errors, for if they shared the same views, they would agree that there are no errors. As a matter of fact, the determination of E3 or E4 can never be completely unbiased, because it depends fundamentally on the belief system and values of whoever is making the determination. For this reason we would not expect everyone to come to the same conclusion. In fact, the real purpose of E3 and E4 are often to elicit differences in values and beliefs. This flips E3 and E4 on their heads. That is, once one has committed E3 and E4 errors, if one is reflective and thus able to see and admit one's errors, one can then work backward using E3 and E4 to pinpoint differences in underlying values.

To be fair, Type Four Errors span the entire ideological and political spectrum. No single party or point of view has a monopoly on them. For example, during the 2008 Democratic primaries, many of the criticisms leveled by Senators Clinton and Obama against each other were clearly disingenuous. To say that both candidates were guilty of committing E3s and E4s is putting it mildly.

We would not be honest if we did not admit openly that we share a particular point of view or bias. Both of the authors are progressives in a basic sense that is made abundantly clear by George Lakoff.[17] We believe that the protection and empowerment of those who are less fortunate are two of the fundamental moral duties of government. For this reason, if we are more critical of conservatives, it is because along with Lakoff we believe that in the past thirty years conservatives have so dominated the political landscape and skewed our political vocabulary that a correction is long overdue. In our terms, a correction of Type Four Errors is needed.

Nonetheless, Lakoff also helps to pinpoint critical defects in liberal or progressive thinking. Liberals and progressives are trapped by the general assumptions of the Enlightenment. They believe that people are moved and persuaded primarily by rational arguments that are devoid of emotion. In doing this, they are often oblivious to the fact that people are moved by emotion, not by cold, hard facts and logic alone. This does not mean that reason and logic are irrelevant (if they were, then why write this book?); but unless they are accompanied by the "right" appeals to emotion, then they fall mainly on deaf ears and minds.

No better example of the failure of liberals to comprehend the importance of emotions in politics could be given than the July 21,

2008, cover of the *New Yorker*. On the cover is a cartoon of Barack Obama dressed as a Muslim extremist and his wife, Michelle, dressed as an Angela Davis-type terrorist touching their fists in a parody of their spontaneous celebration after winning the Democratic nomination. Off to the side is a partially obscured but nonetheless clearly recognizable picture of Osama bin Laden hanging on the wall while in the fireplace an American flag is burning.

In defending the cartoon, the magazine used the excuse that it was merely a "satire" of the innuendos and outright lies of conservatives that Senator Obama was really a Muslim extremist. The intent, therefore, was to bring those lies to the surface by parodying them. (The cartoon was entitled by its creator, Barry Blitt, "The Politics of Fear.")

Although we naturally defend the rights of the editors to print anything they choose, and furthermore we recognize that satire is never popular or timely, we think that at best the editors were extremely naive if they believed that satire could ever be justified by rational arguments alone. We also don't believe that satire can ever be fully decoupled from the charged emotions of the times, but then it is precisely the purpose of satire to provoke strong emotions on both sides. If that was indeed the intention of the editors, they succeeded admirably; but they also succeeded in giving conservatives the best iconic image they could have for spreading further damaging lies against Senator Obama. Were they thereby solving the right or the wrong problem precisely? We leave it for the reader to judge.

Interestingly enough, a few days later the Sunday, July 20, 2008, edition of the *New York Times* reprinted a counter satire by Patrick O'Connor of the *Los Angeles Daily News*. It was a parody of the cover of the *New Yorker*. It showed President Bush and Vice President Cheney dressed in the same costumes as Barack and Michelle Obama. However, in this cartoon a picture of Richard Nixon replaced that of Osama bin Laden, and a burning copy of the U.S. Constitution replaced the American flag. Obviously which cartoon one finds offensive depends on one's political point of view.

Are the two cartoons thereby equal? We don't believe so. The *New Yorker* cartoon is offensive for portraying what has been *falsely implied* about Barack and Michelle Obama, not to mention for the racial and ethnic stereotypes it employs, while the Bush and Cheney cartoon is offensive because of the *actual deeds* of President Bush and Vice President Cheney. Instead of dispelling the lies about Barack Obama, the *New Yorker* cartoon inflames them—but then this is the charge that is typically leveled against satire. Of course supporters of President Bush and Vice President Cheney can contend the same.

More important, however, is that by exploiting and inflaming our emotions, both of the cartoons divert us from the real problems facing America: the need for deep structural changes in the system as a whole. In a word, we need to change the underlying rules of the game.

Finally, as we argue at the end of Chapter Five, the original *New Yorker* cartoon may not actually qualify as satire in that it did not go far enough. In short, it was not outrageous enough. It was merely an example of stereotyping.

CONCLUDING REMARKS

Two very strong conclusions emerge already from our brief introduction to Errors of the Third and Fourth Kinds:

1. Never, ever trust a single definition or a single formulation of an important problem. If anyone promises or offers you a single definition of an important problem, then if you can, run as fast and as far way from that person, organization, society, and so on as you are able. If you can't run, and if you are able, then make a strong stand and fight. Do everything in your power to resist the definition.

2. A single person or organization by itself cannot determine whether it is committing an E3 or E4.

If we are never to trust a single definition or a single formulation of an important problem, then it is clear that our basic notions of strength and leadership will have to change drastically, if not radically. We will have to learn not merely to tolerate but to relish having our most basic beliefs and assumptions challenged. We will have to accept the notion that presenting more than one agreed-upon definition of a problem is a strength, not a weakness. We will have to see it as a fundamental attribute of leadership.

Needless to say, we are far from such an ideal. None of the current candidates for president in the last election would have survived for long by implementing such a principle. Still, because of his personality and training as a law school professor, President Obama is more inclined than most to tolerate and practice such a principle.

We will also have to revise our notions of what it means to be objective. The fact is that the determination of what are Errors of the Third and Fourth Kinds is not and could never be fully ethically and politically neutral, that is, acceptable to everyone no matter what their political persuasion and belief system. We can never expect everyone to agree fully, or even partially, with our determinations. (As we show later, this is not true even in science.) But if we can show that this fact in itself is a strength rather than a weakness, then we will have accomplished one of our most important aims. We will have elevated our disagreements to a higher level, not necessarily removed them. In this way we can learn from our disagreements, not dismiss them out of hand.

To lessen our natural, inborn propensity to commit Errors of the Third and Fourth Kinds, we will also have to mature far beyond our current state of human development and evolution.

Whether we eventually mature or not, one thing is clear: our ability to survive, let alone prosper, in a complex and dangerous world depends more and more on our ability to know and challenge our basic assumptions, and hence to solve the right problems precisely:

> At least five of the eight suspects in the failed terrorist attacks in London and Glasgow, Scotland, were identified as doctors from Iraq, Jordan, Lebanon, and India, while staff at a Glasgow hospital said two others were a doctor and a medical student.

"It sends rather a chill down the spine to think that people's values can be so perverted," said Pauline Neville-Jones, former head of the Joint Intelligence Committee, which advises the British government.

"It means obviously that you can't make any assumptions, or have any preconceptions about the kind of people who might become terrorists. It does mean that you widen the net, obviously," she said on BBC-TV.[18]

We couldn't disagree more. Of necessity, one can't help but make all kinds of assumptions. The world is too complex to know everything for certain before one acts, including this very statement. Instead, what we need to do is speed up the recognition and critique of our basic assumptions and not assume that we can get away with making no assumptions at all. The assumption that you can't make any assumptions is itself too big, too general, too powerful, and too wrong an assumption to make.

An article in *TIME* magazine on the Virginia Tech massacre put it even stronger:

Detectives and military people have a saying about their line of work: "Assumption is the mother of all f___ups." . . . Students told police a gunman had been going from room to room looking for his girlfriend. *Assuming* they were dealing with a lovers' quarrel, police secured the murder scene and began gathering evidence. The crime was over, the investigation begun, or so they thought.[19]

THE ASSUMPTIONS WE MAKE are literally a matter of life and death.

We can't solve old and new problems with the assumptions, mindsets, and institutions of the past.

2 WHAT IS A PROBLEM?
An Initial Framework for
Type Three and Type Four Errors

Something is a problem if and only if it is a member of the set of all other problems.

—C. WEST CHURCHMAN

[People] are not confronted with problems that are independent of each other, but with dynamic situations that consist of complex systems of changing problems that interact with each other. . . . I call such situations messes. Problems are abstractions extracted from *messes* by analysis. . . . [1]

Therefore, when a mess, which is a system of problems, is taken apart, it loses its essential properties and so does each of its parts. The behavior of a mess depends more on how the treatment of its parts interact than how they act independently of each other. *A partial solution to a whole system of problems is better than whole solutions of each of its parts taken separately.*[2]

EXERCISES VERSUS PROBLEMS

The difficulty—dare we say problem—with most discussions of problems is that we think we already know what problems are, let alone what *problems* are facing us. A good part of this misconception is due to the *mis*education system.

From grammar school through college—and beyond—we are not taught the differences between exercises and problems. Over and over again the impression is conveyed that they are the same, but they are not.

For instance, "If Billy has saved $6 and he needs $11 to buy a game, how much more money does he need to save?" is a simple *word exercise*. It is not a problem. For this reason, calling it a word problem is not only fundamentally misleading but also plain wrong.

Characteristics of Exercises

1. *Exercises are preformulated so that the student does not have to undertake the difficult task of determining what the problem is in the first place.* What are the boundaries of the problem? What are the context and the environment within which it exists? What variables drawn from which discipline or disciplines will be used to frame the problem? Whom does the problem affect? How serious is it for whom? In other words, so what? What's riding on the solution? Who cares?

For example, if we were asked to find all of the legitimate ways in which Billy could raise the extra money he needs to buy a game, and the particular ways that were applicable to his life situation, then we would have a true problem, not an exercise in arithmetic or simple algebra. Merely knowing that Billy needs to obtain an additional $5 tells us nothing about how he can actually go about obtaining it. Are Billy and his family poor? Does all the money he earns go to helping his family eat? If so, then the problem is how to help a family that is struggling financially to keep itself afloat. Arithmetic is of little help in solving this problem. A more relevant approach might be financial counseling for the whole family.

This is not to say that learning how to do exercises is totally unimportant. To the contrary, it is merely to say that regardless of how, and how well, they are taught, simple exercises are not the same as problems.

By calling the exercise about Billy preformulated, we mean not only that the exercise is unambiguous, but that all of the information necessary to solve it is completely specified. In other words, everything confusing and extraneous has been removed. As a result, the student does not learn how to formulate and solve problems in the midst of confusion and noise, that is, surrounded by extraneous and contradictory information.

For instance, suppose that every time Billy counts his money he comes up with a different result. What should the student conclude? That Billy doesn't know how to count? That's one possibility, but only one. There are many others, such as one of his siblings is "borrowing" money from him with or without his knowledge, or he has a "leaky" piggy bank or pants pocket.

This is precisely the trouble with most textbooks and with education in general. The mistaken assumption is that by giving students a steady diet of preformulated exercises, we will help them formulate and solve real, complex problems. Instead, it often only makes them want more of the same.

Another mistaken and largely implicit assumption is that real, complex problems can generally be decomposed into a series of simple and independent exercises, and thus that the solution to the original problem is the *sum of the solutions to the separate exercises.* As the quote from Ackoff that opens this chapter argues, however, a problem is the *product of the interactions among the parts* that make up a mess. That is, not only are problems parts of messes, but they also cannot be separated from them because they do not exist apart from them. Thus the solution, if there is one, is highly interactive as well. In short, the solution is a function of the mess as a whole, not of any one of its parts.

2. *Exercises have one and only one solution.* In the exercise about Billy the solution is $5. This is one of the things that makes this an exercise rather than a problem. Exercises thus convey the false impression that all problems have a single formulation, and as a result, a single solution.

3. *Once they are solved, exercises* remain *solved.* They are solved for everyone everywhere who understands the rules of the game—in the exercise about Billy, elementary arithmetic or simple algebra. Furthermore, everyone who understands arithmetic and

algebra should get the same answer: $5. (This fact helps to explain the simpleminded assertion that math and science are the only truly universal languages. A more accurate but no less dubious assertion is that exercises are universal.)

4. *Exercises are usually the province of a single discipline.* Every discipline has its own preferred textbooks. Rarely do textbooks from different disciplines share the same problems. To solve shared problems, the student would have to integrate and apply knowledge from two separate disciplines or fields simultaneously.

5. *Exercises instill another false lesson:* An activity is not a problem unless it can be defined clearly, precisely, and unambiguously, and *prior* to one's working on it. Also, the definition is not supposed to vary as one works on the problem. So, not only is the definition supposed to be constant but it is also supposed to be articulated prior to the solution.

The result of teaching only exercises is that students are turned into "certainty junkies." Anyone with teaching experience knows that students rebel like mad if they are given problems when they have been conditioned to expect exercises.

Problems have none of these characteristics. For example, questions such as "Should the United States have invaded Iraq?" and "How should the United States extricate itself from Iraq?" are, to put it mildly, tortuous problems, not simpleminded exercises.

Characteristics of Problems

1. *Problems are not pre-formulated.* One of the biggest difficulties with problems is determining exactly what the problem is. Problem formulation is one of the most crucial aspects of problem solving. As an old saying puts it, "A problem well put is half solved," and (we paraphrase) "He or she who controls the problem-setting agenda of a nation controls its destiny."

2. *Problems have more than one solution because they have more than one formulation.* As Iraq illustrates only too painfully, people with opposing political perspectives and ideologies don't see issues in the same way. Indeed, why should we expect them to?

3. *Unlike exercises, problems are dynamic.* They not only change as the circumstances change, but they also change in response to our so-called solutions. More often than not the solutions not only contribute to the problems but actually make them worse. For instance, the war in Iraq has made the Middle East more unstable, not more stable.

4. *Problems are not the exclusive province of any single discipline or profession.* For instance, we would not expect an economist and a psychologist to have the same definition of the 2008 financial crisis.

5. *Problems are inherently "messy."* Take away the messiness and you take away what makes them problems.

Embedded in this fifth characteristic is another important difference between exercises and problems: *More often than not the definition of the problem emerges only at the end of an inquiry, not at the beginning.* If one really knew the definition of the problem prior to working on it, then it's not a true problem. The common admonitions to define the problem precisely and not vary the definition of the problem are, strictly speaking, complete nonsense.

Problems such as Iraq and the financial crisis are not well-defined, clear-cut, and independent of each other. Rather, they are huge entangled webs that are interconnected in complex and myriad ways.

In short, complex problems such as Iraq and the financial crisis are mega-crises on top of mega-messes, according to Russell Ackoff, who defines a *mess* as a system of problems in which no single problem exists apart from the entire mess of which it is a part.[3]

As we show in Chapter Eight, concepts such as God, religion, and spirituality do not have single, well-defined meanings and definitions. They are grasped, if only in part, by being lived as a member of a community. As a result, they cannot be captured fully in static definitions. Indeed, why should we expect complex ideas to have single meanings?

TWO DECEPTIVELY SIMPLE PROBLEMS

To make the discussion more concrete and to explore the ideas further, we offer here two deceptively simple examples that we have used repeatedly to stimulate the thinking of students and of the participants in the workshops and seminars we have conducted on complex problem solving. These real-life examples illustrate how easy it is to commit Type Three and Type Four Errors.

The Elevator Problem

The manager of a large high-rise office building was receiving mounting complaints about poor elevator service. She decided to call in a consultant to advise her on what to do to solve the problem.

This short description of the problem is all we give the participants. At this point we stop the presentation and ask them who they would call as a consultant. We also ask them to list as many assumptions as they can that they have made when calling a particular kind of consultant.

Most people instinctively call in an elevator engineer or repairperson of some kind. In doing so, they are assuming implicitly that *the problem is fundamentally in the building* and that *it is a physical problem* (shades of the Coca-Cola executives discussed in Chapter One).

The difficulty with this formulation of the problem is that the solutions recommended by an elevator engineer—such as putting in new elevators or staggering them so that some elevators go only as high as the first twenty floors, and so forth—are generally so expensive that it is almost worthwhile to tear down the whole building and rebuild it from scratch.

Fortunately, one of the tenants in the building was a psychologist. She ascertained that the waiting times for the elevators were not appreciably longer than in comparable buildings nearby. She suggested a much cheaper solution. She recommended that mirrors be placed in the lobby so that people could occupy themselves while waiting. The psychologist assumed that the problem might be in the people, not in the building. (Today we would place huge TV screens in the lobby, so that people could watch CNN, or even a coffee bar. We might even suggest brief yoga and meditation exercises, thereby defining the problem as "spiritual"!)

The elevator problem illustrates clearly what it means to solve the wrong problem precisely. In this case, the "wrong" solution is the alternative that is far more expensive than the "right" solution. Notice, however, that *right* and *wrong* can take on many different meanings depending on how the problem is defined in the first place. For instance, the key phrase "receiving mounting numbers of complaints about poor elevator service" was purposefully left vague and ill-defined. Suppose that the mounting complaints were coming from only one or two of the building's most powerful tenants? If so, then the problem might have been primarily political. It certainly had a strong political element, that is, how to keep the powerful happy and content. However, what if, as a result of placating the most powerful tenants, the rest of the tenants had banded together in opposition? It could then be both a legal and a political problem.

In contrast to exercises, real problems have as many formulations as there are disciplines and professions. Also, once the problem was defined as needing to place mirrors in the lobby, then it literally became a straightforward exercise in selecting the right sizes and placement of the mirrors.

The next example is literally a problem of life and death. Once again, it shows that everything depends on the assumptions we make about a situation.

The World War II Airplane Problem

During the early phases of World War II, British and U.S. airplanes were being shot down at unacceptably high rates. British and U.S. Army senior officers decided to strengthen the planes by putting more armor plating on them. However, the armor plating could not be applied everywhere indiscriminately, because the planes would then be too heavy to fly.

A bright young engineer got the clever idea of making life-size mockups of the planes and putting pencil marks everywhere the planes had received a bullet hole. How did the engineer use what he saw as a guide to where to apply the armor plating?

In giving your answer, what assumptions are you making? List as many assumptions as you can that influenced your answer. What if your assumptions are wrong? How would this affect your answer?

As with the elevator problem, we typically divide people up into small groups of no more that six or eight people so they can interact more easily; we then give them no more than fifteen minutes to discuss the problem. In every class or workshop we have conducted, at least one person has gotten the "right" answer.

The engineer reasoned as follows:

I am only seeing the bullet holes in the planes that have made it safely back to base. I am not seeing the bullet holes in the planes that did not make it back. Therefore, I recommend that we put the armor where we are not seeing bullet holes.

Of course the engineer could have been wrong. Only time would tell if his assumptions were correct. But notice what he did. He flipped the common, taken-for-granted assumption on its head. The typical assumption was, put more armor where the bullet holes are. The engineer reasoned instead, put the armor where there are no bullet holes.

Of course this assumption does not rule out entirely that some combination of placing the armor where the bullet holes were and where they were not would lower substantially the rate at which planes were being shot down. Perhaps certain planes were not making it back because of the characteristics of certain pilots. The "correct" solution then would be a combination of psychology and technology.

Whatever the solution is, if indeed there ever is a final one, both of these "simple" examples demonstrate unequivocally the importance of the assumptions we make about a situation.

THE MOST GENERAL DEFINITION OF A PROBLEM

A problem exists when a set of presumably ethical means (such as for putting armor plating on a plane) for achieving a desired set of presumably ethical ends (such as safeguarding pilots in WWII) is not clear and we want to find or create those means. A *well-structured problem* is one for which the means and the ends are easily known or can be specified. In addition, one's ethical stance and values are also well-known and accepted by a "significant body" of stakeholders. In this case, the problem is the need to determine which of the means are the most efficient—that is, least costly, involving the least amount of time and effort, and so on—in attaining the desired ends. Thus, a *well-structured problem* is nearly, but not completely, equivalent to an exercise.

In contrast, an *ill-structured problem* is one for which the means or the ends or both are unknown (or the effectiveness of which are in doubt) or for which sharp and significant disagreement exists over what means should be employed to achieve what ends. In addition, one's ethical stance and values are in doubt or not well accepted by a significant body of stakeholders. The problem is to determine the nature of the problem, that is, how to formulate it.

The most extreme example of an ill-structured problem is a *wicked problem*.[4] (Iraq more than fits the bill.) A wicked problem is one for which there appears to be no satisfactory way of determining an appropriate set of means or ends that would obtain sufficient agreement among a diverse set of stakeholders. That is, no currently known discipline, profession, or body of knowledge is sufficient to define the "wicked," complex nature of the problem.

Type Three and Type Four Errors are inevitable features of anything worthy of the name *problem*, because, first, in general we wouldn't expect everyone to have and pursue the same ends. Second, we wouldn't expect everyone to select and use the same means. Third, we wouldn't expect everyone to agree on what's most effective. Fourth, and most critical of all, we wouldn't expect everyone to agree on the definition of what's ethical.

In a fundamental sense, all problems that are worthy of the name have significant aspects or elements that are ill-structured. This fact alone gives rise to one of the most interesting forms of Type Three and Type Four Errors: *saying that a problem is well-structured when it is actually ill-structured.* Politicians are always trying to convince us that this is the case. When a situation like this happens, they and we try to divert our attention from the real problem by focusing our energies on exercises. In this way we attempt to lower the anxiety associated with real problems.[5]

Also, there is a big difference between *means problems* and *ends problems.* In the former, presumably the ends are well-known and accepted. The problem is then to discover or create the most efficient means for obtaining the ends (for instance, the most efficient means of overturning Saddam Hussein). Such problems are termed *efficient means problems.* In ends problems, one is charged with discovering or creating a set of ends around which people can coalesce. Such problems are best termed *existential problems,* because the ends give meaning and purpose to those who are pursuing them. This is true even if the ends can never be fully attained. For instance, although we cannot eliminate wars at the present time, and perhaps never will, we still ascribe to the ideal of finally eliminating all wars from the human condition. (An *ideal* is an end that we can never fully attain but that we can hopefully approach indefinitely. Indeed, ideals exist to give us meaning, purpose, and hope.)

Confusing means and ends problems is one of the most significant forms of Type Three and Type Four Errors. That is, labeling something as a means problem when it is an ends problem, and vice versa, is obviously an important error.

THE VERB "TO SOLVE" AND SEVERAL RELATED VERBS

Because most of us have been "trained," not "educated," on exercises, we also think we know what it means to "solve" a problem; but problems do not have the same kinds of solutions as exercises do. To see this, let's take a look at the verb *to solve* and several related verbs.

Suppose a problem, *P*, exists whenever there is a significant gap between *I*, what we ideally would like to accomplish, and *A*, what we can currently accomplish. Thus, $P = I - A > 0$. That is, a problem exists whenever P (the difference between our ideals, I, and our current abilities, A) is greater than zero.

Refer back to the simple example of Billy, who has $6 but needs $5 more in order to buy a game costing $11. In this case, I = $11 and A = $6. Thus, P = $5. However, in terms of our earlier discussion, by itself P = $5 is not the problem. How to raise the $5, not the amount itself, is the problem.

To "solve" P means to make P = 0, that is, I = A. We can do this in two ways: either by raising A to I or by lowering I to A. In the first case, we *raise* our actual abilities (means) to our ideals (ends). In the second case, we *lower* our ideals to our abilities.

Strictly speaking, only exercises and well-structured problems have solutions in which P = 0. Ill-structured and wicked problems do not have such solutions. They are "coped with" and "managed," but never fully solved.

To *resolve* a problem means to contain it within acceptable limits. For example, we accept unemployment within the range of 4 to 6 percent. We no longer insist that P = 0, but we insist instead that P be bounded within acceptable limits. According to economists, in the case of unemployment, to attempt to make P = 0 would be to create even worse economic and social problems.

To *dissolve* a problem means to lower or redefine its importance. When we dissolve a problem, we say that other problems within the system (the mess) in which the problem exists deserve our attention more. (Recall that Ackoff defines a *mess* as a system of problems in which no single problem exists apart from the entirety of which it is a part.[6]) P still exists within acceptable limits, but we shift our attention to other problems. The problem can be managed properly only by managing other problems within the mess.

To *absolve* a problem means to accept that P may never fully vanish. It may even grow worse over time. At best, it waxes and wanes. For example, it means accepting that problems such as terrorism are not *wars* that can be won but rather *social diseases or pathologies* that can only be managed as best we can over time.

The real essence of absolving, however, is as follows: more often than not we are committed to a pet solution or a series of pet solutions. In absolving, we work backward from our pet solution to the definition of a problem that is compatible with our preferred solution, but we do it in such a way that we make it appear that the definition of the problem came first.

As we show in the coming chapters, these related verbs are crucial, because we always have to decide which problems, in our best judgment, can be solved rather than resolved, dissolved, or absolved. Many Type Three and Type Four Errors occur when we attempt to solve problems that can only be resolved, dissolved, or absolved.

AN INITIAL FRAMEWORK FOR PROBLEM FORMULATION
Here we present a framework for differentiating between varied political positions and ideologies. Rooted in the works of George Lakoff and Ken Wilber, this framework can be used to understand how, where, when, and why Type Three and Type Four Errors arise.[7]

The basic distinction between political orientations is between liberals on the Left and conservatives on the Right. Their views of the world—that is, their worldviews—are so fundamentally and dramatically different from each other that for all practical purposes the United States has been in a protracted cultural civil war for the last thirty years or so.

To a significant extent, liberals and conservatives no longer seriously engage with one another. Instead, with increasing anger, ferocity, and vile, they shout and talk past one another. Their views have become so hardened and coarse as the result of recent events and the posturing of extremists on both sides of the political spectrum that it is almost impossible to find anyone who does not come to an important issue or problem with rigid preset views. In short, both sides thoroughly demonize the other.[8] Consider, for example, poverty and welfare.

The Right mainly views poverty as the failure of individuals. The poor are poor because they either are lazy or don't have the values that would motivate them to find work, however humble and poorly paid it might be. In brief, it's entirely up to the individual, not the government, to work his or her way out of poverty. Welfare only breeds dependence, lack of self-reliance, and ultimately feelings of low self-worth.

The Left mainly views poverty as the failure of government, or the state. The poor are poor because of racism and other societal forces that make it literally impossible for individuals to make it on their own without substantial help from the government. It's one of the major responsibilities of government to help people work their way out of poverty. Welfare is not a handout but a fundamental right.

As George Lakoff has pointed out, conservatives are governed by the psychology of the Stern Father, of whom Hobbes is the representative philosopher.[9] According to this view, the world is a very hard and mean place. If you don't play by the rules, you deserve to be punished. If you don't punish children when they break the rules, they will not grow up to respect rules and be able to fend for themselves.

Liberals have a completely different philosophy. They are governed by the psychology of the Nurturing Mother, of whom Rousseau is the representative philosopher. According to this view, children need love and care if they are to develop into responsible adults. Instead of being punished harshly when they inevitably break the rules, they need to be taught to respect the rights of others by first developing respect for themselves. If we don't help them do this, we will never produce healthy and responsible citizens.

Both views are profoundly right and wrong. Again, it's a both-and, not an either/or, situation. Ideally, parents should be a combination of the Nurturing Mother and the Stern Farther. Children need to be taught to obey rules, but in a caring and loving manner. Without the Stern Father, the Nurturing Mother turns into the Indulgent Mother; and without the Nurturing Mother, the Stern Father turns into the Autocratic and Abusive Father or Parent.

If we were able to integrate both sides of the spectrum, we might just be able to forge a new way of looking at our problems. We might be able to go from being either totally independent of or totally dependent on others to being interdependent.

CONCLUDING REMARKS

A strong conclusion follows almost directly from the preceding framework. Liberals and conservatives engage equally in absolving problems. Their respective ideologies function as pet hypotheses from which they derive not only their solutions to important problems but, even more fundamentally, their definitions of problems. Conservatives believe strongly in solving problems, that is, they believe that each problem has one solution. In contrast, liberals believe just as strongly in resolving and dissolving, that is, in the notion that important problems always have more than one solution.

In the coming chapters we show that many of our most crucial problems—and especially the fundamental errors we make in misconstruing them—stem from the ideas we have discussed in this chapter. It is almost impossible to exaggerate just how obsessed Western societies are with exercises and well-structured problems. We take it for granted that one doesn't really know something until one can reduce it to precise definitions and break it apart into supposedly independent problems. In short, analysis is king:

The place to go looking for longer life is in the repair shop.

One man who has done just that is Aubrey de Grey, who is an independent researcher working in Cambridge, England, a man who provokes strong opinions. He is undoubtedly a visionary . . . for he believes that anti-ageing technology could come about in a future that many now alive might live to see.

Vision or mirage, Dr. de Grey has defined the problem precisely. Unlike most workers in the field, he has an engineering background, and is thus ideally placed to look into the biological repair shop. As he sees things, ageing has seven components; deal with all seven, and you stop the process in its tracks. . . .

It is quite a shopping list. But it does, at least, break the problem into manageable parts. . . . [10]

One has to have a very simple view of the world indeed to believe that by defining the problem precisely and breaking it down into manageable parts one will thereby unlock the secrets of ageing. Thank God that the world is not so simple!

3   ORGANIZED MEANNESS

The Biggest and Most Broken

Health System in the World

To understand quality improvement, start with a simple observation: You get what you pay for. . . . We want the medical system to improve our health, but we reimburse it for treating us when we're sick. Medical care is not the same as health improvement, and the system does poorly when they differ. A better medical system would pay for health improvement, rather than for provision of service.[1]

Cost containment is not a goal in itself. Increasing the value of the system is. The right step is to move toward a system that improves our health, spending less as appropriate but more if need be. We can move forward on this, but we must think differently than we have.[2]

THE BEST MEDICAL SYSTEM
VERSUS THE BEST HEALTH CARE SYSTEM

Former New York City mayor and 2008 Republican presidential candidate Rudolph Giuliani, politicians from both parties, and even health care experts who should know better have long contended that the United States has the best health care system in the world. The evidence overwhelmingly supports a very different conclusion. From the standpoint of technical capabilities, and only from that standpoint, the United States has the best *medical* system in the world. However, from the standpoint of access and of the general health of the population, the United States does *not* have the best *health care* system. Advanced medical technology and the delivery of health care are not the same thing. In fact, it is even more true to say that the United States has a *mediocre sick care system.*

The United States does not have the best health care system, because lack of access and coverage are a huge problem for millions of uninsured and underinsured Americans. There are even huge problems for those who have medical insurance but are routinely denied access to the very care for which they and their employers have paid. In short, *solving the problem of how to produce the best medical care for those who can afford it is not the same as solving the problem of how to provide the best health care for all Americans who increasingly are unable to afford it and are denied access to it.* This is the primary Type Four Error that this chapter discusses.

Pointing to a scar on his head, then Democratic senator and vice presidential candidate Joe Biden[3] once remarked, "Doctors gave me back my life. They repaired aneurysms in an artery that was bleeding into my brain. Without their care, the aneurysms would have either killed or seriously impaired me." Senator Biden was "given back his life" because he had access to the system. Far too many of us do not.

According to Kevin Lamb of the *New York Times* and the Organization for Economic Cooperation and Development, in 2004 the U.S. medical system cost $6,102 per patient, or twice the spending of nineteen of the twenty-nine developed countries.[4] Between 2000 and 2006, U.S. medical insurance premiums rose by 58.5 percent after inflation. In sharp contrast, wages increased by only 1.7 percent.

Referring to a Commonwealth Fund Commission survey that compared health care in six countries—the United States, Canada, the United Kingdom, Australia, New Zealand, and Germany—Lamb notes that the United States ranks last in access, equity, efficiency, safe care, and living long, healthy, and productive lives.[5] Writing in the *Journal of the American Medical Association*, Dr. Ezekiel

Emanuel put it bluntly, "If a politician declares that the United States has the best health care system in the world today, [then] he or she [is] clueless."[6] The Commonwealth Fund Commission survey also found that U.S. doctors rank last among five English-speaking countries in listening, explaining, and spending enough time with their patients.[7]

The American public and the American medical profession are not totally unaware of these and other deficiencies. So how come the richest country in the world cannot meet the medical needs of a sizeable portion of its citizens?

THREE FUNDAMENTAL AND TAKEN-FOR-GRANTED ASSUMPTIONS

Three fundamental and largely taken-for-granted assumptions drive the American medical system. As we saw in Chapter One, faulty or misguided assumptions are the source of virtually all Type Three and Type Four Errors. Indeed, every assumption not only is an implicit definition of some important problem, but also, as a result, implicitly contains the solution. In other words, it is a very short step from assumptions to problems, solutions, and errors. For this reason, in this chapter we examine each of the following assumptions in depth, including how each has led to a skewed definition of the problem with health care, and hence how each is a Type Four Error.

1. *Government is the problem.* This idea was the core of the so-called Reagan revolution in the 1980s. Although Reagan was referring primarily to the welfare system, the fundamental philosophical principle behind his conviction was the strongly held belief that the government has no business providing a safety net for its citizens. This philosophy has permeated American health care ever since, and perhaps did so even well before. As we show later, the data do not support this contention.

2. *Universal health care is too costly; the American economy cannot afford it.* Since the 1970s, cost cutting has been the main vehicle, and objective, for attempting the efficient and rational delivery of health care. We show not only that this assumption is too

narrow and limiting, but also that the data do not support it. In fact, it has led to an irrational and abusive pricing system.

3. *The unregulated free market is the best if not the only way to deliver health care to American citizens.* The concept of an unfettered market is promoted by economists—many of whom are disciples of Nobel Prize-winning economist Milton Friedman—at the University of Chicago, and elsewhere. Evidence worldwide does not support the claim that an unregulated free market is necessary or best for the delivery of a comprehensive health care plan.

1. Government as the Problem

The basic assumption that the government should not play a role in providing access to health care for all of its citizens underlies many, if not most, of the decisions currently being made about the U.S. medical system. In contrast, most of the Western European nations, such as France, Germany, and Switzerland, long ago concluded that the best way to maintain the overall health of their citizens is for the government to run health care. In spite of the fact that these countries obviously have unique features dictated by their distinctive histories and particular cultures, none of their citizens are denied access to medical care. Nonetheless, in an extremely well-researched book, *Redefining Health Care*, Michael Porter, professor of management at the Harvard Business School, and Elizabeth Olmsted Teisberg of the University of Virginia strongly criticize the notion that government should be the gatekeeper and primary provider of health care.[8]

Porter and Teisberg contend that government is basically too bureaucratic to be creative, innovative, and competitive. As a result, it is unable to hold down costs. The only way to do so is to have unconstrained competition in the so-called free market. In short, government is fundamentally incapable of providing efficient and meaningful health care to the American public. Consequently, with few exceptions, the management of health care is best left to private industry. In effect, Porter and Teisberg argue, having government provide and administer health care is the wrong solution to the wrong problem.

Through the use of highly selective information, conservatives and think-tank intellectuals have continually promoted the argument that health care is best left to private industry. The claim is made over and over again that government inhibits innovation, limits and prevents choice, delays or denies treatment, provides inefficient care, and in the absence of competition is too costly. The advancement of such claims has been accompanied by the use of explosive terminology such as *socialized medicine*, thus scaring the public with the fear of dictatorial government control. Indeed, for most of its history, the American Medical Association (AMA) has staunchly resisted and actively fought virtually all attempts to provide broader health care for the American public by calling it socialism.

The data do not substantiate these claims and other assumptions about government-sponsored health care. Although the highly selective use of information certainly points out problems associated with government management, it also ignores or minimizes the problems presented by the current system.

The bureaucracy and the micromanagement of health care decisions associated with the current private-payer system, in which physicians and other health care professionals are constantly harassed and exhausted by the paperwork and administrative overhead necessary to meet the regulations imposed by the insurance industry, are as bad as anything imaginable with government-sponsored health care. Consider the case of Dr. Alice Linder, a board-certified pediatrician and psychiatrist. Dr. Linder is medical director of a large children's mental health agency in northern New York State. She has to work through the insurance industry to prescribe and obtain drugs for the young people who patronize her practice. One of the problems she faces is that many of the drugs she would prescribe are not on the insurance companies' formulary lists, even though they are the appropriate and standard way of treating the problems her patients face. Dr. Linder has to fill out countless forms and make repeated telephone calls to try to obtain the proscribed treatments.

The insurance companies also parcel out mental health treatments a few sessions at a time and require repeated paperwork in order to continue treatment. All of this paperwork takes significant time away from treatment, and costs lots of money. This is just one example of the countless problems that physicians face daily with the current private health insurance system.

In contrast, government programs such as Medicare and the Veterans Health Administration (VA) actually minimize administrative and bureaucratic costs. The administrative costs of Medicare are estimated to be 2 percent of its total costs whereas the administrative costs of the insurance industry are estimated to be 30 percent. We deal with reasons for this later in the chapter.

The point is that large organizations in both the public and private domains tend to be bureaucratic and to micromanage, that is, to second-guess doctors' decisions, because of their cultures. This has nothing to do, necessarily, with whether the organization is public or private. Medicare and the VA actually have fewer bureaucratic and administrative procedures for micromanaging.

The claim that government limits innovation is also not consistent with the fact that U.S. medical technology is arguably the best in the world. It is a matter of public record that the National Institutes of Health (NIH) are responsible for the development of the most innovative medical research and treatments. As a general rule, industry just can't afford the kinds of high-risk investment that are required. In fact, the vast majority of the great advances in the sciences have come from institutions such as the NIH, the National Science Foundation, the National Aeronautics and Space Administration, and the military establishment.

In sum, the assumption that government is the problem has led us to construct a system in which we pay more for less. In other words, we have solved the (wrong) problem of how to build a system in which private insurers get more by delivering less. This a prime example of one of the biggest Type Four Errors we have ever committed.

2. Cost Cutting

Cost cutting was introduced both as a concept and as a tool in the 1990s in order to minimize the growth of health care costs, which were growing faster than the rate of inflation. Managed care was thought to be the solution because it would cut out the fat in the system. A primary assumption was that neither physicians nor consumers took basic responsibility for holding down the costs of medical care. Consumers were considered to be frivolous in their use of the system. Furthermore, improvements in technology and innovation added substantial costs.

Health maintenance organizations (HMOs) became an increasingly important part of the health care system because managed care was thought of as a good way to control the use of and even to forgo expensive procedures and thereby stop medical costs from spiraling out of control. However, HMOs failed to deliver the expected savings because the whole premise was based on the wrong concept of health care, and even worse, it avoided what should be the true outcome of health care delivery, that is, the general improvement of the health of the population. That is, the problem we ought to be solving is how to improve the general health of the entire population and not just how to hold down and cut costs. Better yet, the correct problem is *how to hold down costs* and *improve the general health of the entire population.*

As flawed as the cost-cutting assumption is, an even more basic assumption has led to solving the wrong problem: that health care is a commodity like any other commodity and not a basic service to which all Americans should have access. The result of this assumption has been the shifting of costs to doctors, hospitals, and patients and away from employers.

It has not generally been recognized that the outcome of the medical system should really be the improvement of health, not necessarily the lowering of costs. Dave Cutler, a well-known health economist at Harvard University, contends that the determination of any improvement in the system should be based on the improvement of care, not on cost cutting per se.[9] Indeed, Cutler has demonstrated that if improvement were viewed as a major desired outcome, then technology and innovation could actually help to lower costs by minimizing utilization of the system, such as reducing the number of hospitalizations.

The development of vaccines for pneumonia, for example, slashed the costs of health care provided to children.[10] Such immunization has reduced related health care costs by 45.3 percent, hospitalization rates due to pneumonia in children by 52.4 percent, and the rates of outpatient visits by 46.9 percent.

In *Redefining Health Care*, Porter and Teisberg point out a fundamental error of cost cutting:

> Thinking regarding cost reduction has been short run, relying on quick hits, such as eliminating expensive drugs or diagnostic procedures, rather than a more fundamental cost reduction over the full cycle of care. True cost can only be measured over the full cycle of care, which begins with prevention and continues through recovery and longer-term management of the condition to limit re-occurrence. The relevant time horizon may be months or even years. What matters for costs is not the cost of any individual intervention or treatment but the overall costs. An expensive drug, a more expensive surgeon, or more spending on rehabilitation may be a bargain over the long run. The right goal is to improve value (the quality of health care per dollar expanded).[11]

In short, cost cutting per se is not systemic. As a result, unless the total costs involved throughout the system are considered, then cost cutting alone is the wrong solution to the wrong problem. It doesn't solve the basic problem of how to provide high-quality care per dollar expended.

Consider type 2 diabetes, a multiphase disease that includes a great many components. The flow chart for patient-integrated disease management in Figure 3.1 depicts all of the components that go into diabetes management.

The treatment of diabetes requires that the doctor communicate adequately with the patient; assess the patient's risk for heart attacks, strokes, and neurological and kidney disease; treat the patient; record the outcome of treatment in a database; and schedule follow-up visits. All of this requires that the patient be seen over a long period.

Dr. Joseph Prendergast runs a diabetes clinic in Palo Alto, Cali-

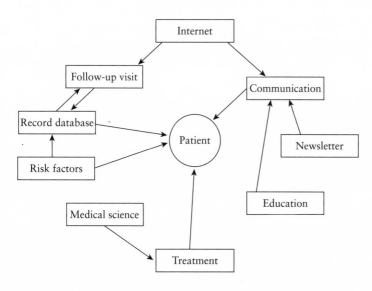

FIGURE 3.1   Flow chart for patient-integrated disease management.
Diagram courtesy of Abraham Silvers.

fornia. He asked Silvers to evaluate the performance of his care. Dr. Prendergast does integrated diabetes management. He has recorded the results of his therapy and stored all of the outcomes of the patient's laboratory values in an electronic database.

Silvers analyzed the data and found that on average the blood sugar concentrations of his patients decreased over the course of treatment, which of course is the desired result. Dr. Prendergast kept tabs on all of the risks that could lead to hospitalization for other problems that could result from unmanaged diabetes. If a patient is not adequately treated, then he or she could eventually be hospitalized for very serious diseases.

The point is, once again, that the costs associated with managed care are a complex phenomenon, and that cost cutting per se, whether indiscriminate or not, is too simplistic a solution. Also, identifying the maintenance of good health as the primary objective of health care provision prevents the serious outcomes that are the reasons for large medical costs. In diabetes, this means hospitalization for heart attacks, kidney failure, or blindness, for example.

In contrast, cost cutting promotes medical costs that are often just plain absurd. *The Wall Street Journal* reported the case of Jim Dawson of Modesto, California, who did everything right.[12] He was gainfully employed and regularly paid his bills, including his medical insurance premiums, on time. Still, he ended up owing California Pacific Medical Center (CPMC), a leading cardiac hospital in San Francisco, more than a million dollars. The hospital padded the bill by marking up the prices for procedures, items, and services. Dr. Pont, CMPC's chief medical officer, admitted that the charges were insane. He stated that "all hospitals operate this way; it's just the basic reality of the industry." According to the *Wall Street Journal*, the bottom line is, "Hospitals say [that] bill padding is their only defense against government and insurer cost cutting, but the practice can leave individuals with wildly inflated bills."

According to the Centers for Disease Control and Prevention, the charges for chronically ill patients account for up to 75 percent of the total spending for health care.[13] Up to 30 percent are the result of the 200 percent increase in obesity over the last twenty years.[14] James Fries, M.D., a former colleague of Silvers at Stanford University, showed that from 1988 to 1989, when retirees practiced good health habits such as weight control, their health care costs were lowered by $372, to $598 per year.[15] In sum, the management of health over the full cycle of care, that is, the systematic and rigorous follow-up and appropriate response to the patients clinical outcomes over time, not cost cutting, is the main issue.

3. The Unregulated Free Market

The assumption that government is the problem has been used to bolster the argument that an unfettered free market is the best if not the only way to address the issue of the delivery of health care. The proponents of unregulated free markets spout the usual arguments championed by Milton Friedman. In brief, the free market system will promote greater competition that in turn will lower costs substantially. Patients will have more choice among health providers and treatment options. The system will be more efficient and will enable consumers to get more for their dollars. The system will also generate innovation that will enhance the health care system. Sadly, the exact opposite has been the case. A few very large insurance companies control the system. As a result, there is actually very little true competition.

The health systems of Western European nations and even those of the U.S. government are actually more cost efficient than the services provided by the big insurance companies. In fact they are more efficient by most measures of efficiency. For example, because the purchase of high-tech equipment is unregulated, U.S. hospitals regularly buy expensive imaging equipment that they use to maintain their competitive edge and attract staff but rarely to treat patients. In sum, people get more choice from Medicare than they get from private insurance plans and from the Medicare advantage plans run by the insurance companies.

According to Dr. Arnold Relman of Harvard University, "medical professionalism in the United States is facing a crisis. Endangered are the ethical foundations of medicine, including the commitment of physicians to put the needs of patients ahead of personal gain, to deal with patients honestly, competently and compassionately and to avoid conflict of interest that could undermine public trust in the altruism of medicine."[16] According to Relman, a major reason for the decline of medical professional values is the growing commercialization of the U.S. health care system.

Nobel Prize-winning economist Kenneth Arrow has stated bluntly that the medical system cannot be defined or treated as a typical market.[17] The concept of supply and demand plays a critical role in the application of free market economics. For instance, supply plays a major role in influencing consumer choice. However, supply and demand cannot play this role in the medical system because decisions have to be based primarily on a patient's condition, that is, on medical needs. In many cases, the patient has only one choice and must therefore make that choice or face dire consequences. As a result, the usual rules for governing business on the basis of supply of services and the demand for profitability do not apply to the health delivery system. In short, health care is *not* like other "products" or "commodities."

THE INSURANCE INDUSTRY

A direct consequence of the three prevailing assumptions—that government is the problem, that cost cutting is an effective device for preventing untold health costs, and that the free market system is the only appropriate approach to health care delivery—which are also Type Four Errors, as we have indicated, has been the promotion and growth of the for-profit insurance industry. As the major gatekeeper for the health care system, the insurance industry is predicated on one model: the idea of the "risk-prone individual." Insurance underwriting is based on avoiding high-risk individuals, or in their vernacular, *adverse populations.*

The prime stakeholders of the industry are not those who pay the premiums but rather the stockholders, that is, the investors. The main goal, therefore, is to maximize profits for the stockholders. Restricting access to medical care claims leads to superprofits. Thus, preventing coverage or denying reimbursement literally "pays." Limiting reimbursements for claims hits the middle-aged population especially hard. Individuals aged fifty to sixty-four who are not covered by employers or group polices have great difficulty getting insurance.[18] They are considered high-risk individuals. The industry naturally hopes that Medicare will cover them when they reach sixty-five.

Stories abound about the denial of insurance. Insurance companies claim that their policies serve to prevent increasing medical costs and to inhibit what is termed *moral hazard*, that is, unlimited free coverage that would cause unnecessary overuse and abuse of the system. However, just the reverse of moral hazard actually occurs. Legitimate claims for individual reimbursement are deliberately and systematically denied. This typically occurs in what is called *post-claims underwriting.* A claim is sent to the insurance company, which the company then investigates, and if the insured is shown to have any vague "preexisting condition," he or she is no longer insured. We call this practice *immoral hazard*, that is, immoral behavior on the part of the insurance industry.

According to the November 10, 2007, edition of the *San Francisco Chronicle*,

Health Net Inc., one of [California's] largest health insurers, tied rewards and savings to its employees' ability to cancel policies based on misrepresentations in members applications, according to documents in a lawsuit against the company. The documents show Health Net saved $35.5 million in "unnecessary" health care expenses for rescinding more than 1,000 policies between 2000 and 2006. At the same time, a Health Net analyst received about $21,000 in bonuses for her work. . . . State regulators and plaintiffs' lawyers have argued that the applications often are vague and confusing. . . . State insurance commissioner Steven Poizner considers the actions taken by Health Net to be "indefensible, immoral and possibly illegal."[19]

In 2007, the California Department of Managed Health Care fined Blue Cross of California $1 million for routinely revoking policies. Other companies in California are being sued for the same reason. Hector De La Torre, a Democratic representative of the fiftieth assembly district, states, "In California, at least six health insurance companies face legal proceedings for canceling policies after patients sought treatment."[20] A large suit has also been filed against Blue Shield. California's insurance commissioner is seeking a $12.6 million penalty against Blue Shield. The December 14, 2007, edition of the *San Francisco Chronicle* stated, "The health insurer unfairly canceled members' medical coverage and improperly processed claims."

In spite of this evidence to the contrary, many still believe that basic reform of the system should be based on the concept that the insurance companies should be the primary gatekeepers for access to health care. In 2007, three of the Republican presidential candidates—Rudolph Giuliani, John McCain, and Fred Thompson—offered medical plans based on this idea.[21] The supreme irony is that under their own proposed medical plans none of them would have received medical insurance because of their preexisting cancer conditions. In addition, the plan proposed by John McCain assumed that financial assistance could be obtained through tax credits, but the average middle-class person making $50,000 a year who pays $15,000 a year in premiums would get only approximately $3,000 in tax relief.[22] They would still have to pay $12,000 in premiums per year, which is unaffordable for a person making that kind of income.

THE DRUG INDUSTRY

In an outstanding book, *The Truth About Drug Companies: How They Deceive Us and What to Do About It*, Marcia Angell, former chief editor of the prestigious *New England Journal of Medicine*, describes the strategies used by the pharmaceutical industry that lead to Type Four Errors.[23] This view of the industry is in sharp contrast to what it used to be—a profitable industry that produced miracle drugs in response to the needs of the general population rather than an industry whose main driving force is to obtain superprofits. Angell discusses the huge costs of prescriptions and the reasons given by the drug industry to justify exorbitant prices.

The pharmaceutical industry is a huge money-making machine, period! To justify their enormous profits, spokespeople for the industry claim over and over that the research necessary for the development of drugs is very expensive. Furthermore, innovation is also very costly. Therefore, if controls were placed on the pricing of drugs, we would all suffer the consequences of not having the life-saving drugs we need.

In direct contradiction, Angell has shown that much of the innovation is done by publicly supported research. She gives many examples of well-known drugs that were initially conceived of not by the drug companies but instead by government-sponsored researchers. The answer that Angell gives to the question of why the prices of drugs are up to two times higher in the United States than they are in Europe is that the major drug companies spend huge amounts to promote their products. According to a report in *Chemical and Engineering News*, the Kaiser Family Foundation found that drug makers spent

$9.2 billion to sell their products in 1996 and $28 billion in 2004.[24] In comparison, $37 billion was spent on research and development.

The drug companies have learned quite well how to solve the problem of convincing us that their enormous profits are justified. Promotional activities often persuade people to ask their doctors for unnecessary or more expensive prescriptions. A study in *JAMA: The Journal of the American Medical Association*, shows that one of the biggest effects on physicians' behavior is requests by patients for brand-name drugs.[25] The government accounting office stated in a report in 2002 that a sizeable number of advertisements were misleading or erroneous.[26] The Food and Drug Administration (FDA) has too few employees to monitor the huge amount of advertising put out by the pharmaceutical industry.

The industry has also engaged in activities that inhibit the introduction of generic drugs. For example, in *evergreening* a company files additional patents on its ongoing drugs by making small changes or adding another existing product to it. This delays the expiration of the patent. Another strategy is to file a *citizen's petition*, which questions the safety of a generic drug while the approval process is in progress. The company may also enter into a deal with a manufacturer of generics to delay the marketing of its drug for several years.

The industry also claims that the cost of the development of drugs has increased considerably. An important factor contributing to increased prices of drugs, it says, is that clinical trials demand longer times than they used to. A recent study published in *Health Affairs* shows that this is not true. An examination of the time it took to develop 168 drugs found that "the median clinical trial and regulatory review periods for drugs approved between 1992 and 2002 were 5.1 months and 1.2 years respectively. Clinical trial periods have not increased during this time frame and regulatory review periods have decreased."[27]

The industry is required to perform post-marketing safety studies, but it is active in minimizing its participation in such studies to evaluate the side effects of drugs. According to the U.S. Government Accountability Office (GAO) in 2002, the industry did not conduct two-thirds of the marketing studies requested by the FDA.[28] Further-more, the drugs moved onto the market too quickly after phase 3 studies, which are final trials to determine the efficacy of a drug. Only a maximum of three thousand patients were used to test the drugs for toxicity. Serious toxicities may take time to occur, and large populations are needed to reveal them. A drug may be distributed to the market after only a few months, which is not necessarily enough time to establish that there are problems with it. Critics claim that the Vioxx fiasco would not have occurred if there had been suffi-cient delays in marketing. (Vioxx was pulled from the market only after it was revealed by an investigative reporter that Merck did not disclose fully its own data showing that the use of Vioxx led to in-creased risk of heart problems for certain patients.)

The number of overseas clinical trials is increasing. The lack of willing patients in the United States is leading to studies in India, Africa, and Eastern Europe, where volunteers are more easily ob-tained. Many of the safety conditions required by the FDA for re-cruiting volunteers are not followed overseas. Some trials do not have informed consent, and some are performed without prior animal studies to help determine the maximum tolerated dose. Sometimes the company does not get approval from the nation in which the trials are conducted even though that country has procedures to as-sess the safety of drugs.[29]

The pharmaceutical companies have engaged in developing so-called *me-too drugs* to take advantage of drugs already on the mar-ket. Many of these studies compare their drugs to placebos instead of to existing drugs that may be just as efficacious or even more so, and possibly much cheaper. The public may be unduly influenced by advertising to ask for a drug that may not be any better and may even be more expensive. An interesting example is the conflict over a drug used for macular degeneration. Ophthalmologists want to use Avastin, a lower-cost drug designed to treat cancer, rather than Lucentis, a drug designed for this condition.[30] Produced by Genen-tech, Avastin costs $40 per injection. Lucentis, or Ranibizumab, also developed by Genentech, costs $2,000 per injection. Genentech tried to inhibit the use of Avastin for macular degeneration through a series of market maneuvers. The uproar over their unethical behavior caused Genentech to change its mind.

THE QUALITY OF CARE

To put it mildly, reducing the quality of care is a gross Type Four Error. The quality of medical care can be defined as the application of best practices—which may be prescribed in the guidelines of medical professional associations or governmental agencies or suggested by the medical literature—in solving a patient's medical problem. We have seen how cost cutting and free markets have diminished the quality of care. The first requirement for quality, obviously, is access to the system. Forty-seven million people have very limited access or no access at all. The second requirement is adequate care. Thirteen million U.S. citizens are underinsured and unable to receive complete treatment. The third requirement is to receive the right treatment. By means of post-claims underwriting, insurance companies have denied reimbursements for treatments prescribed by physicians. Drug company prices are too high for many individuals to receive the right drugs.

Lack of quality care means that many people end up getting unnecessarily sicker; cancer patients may have lower rates of survival than they would otherwise, and procedures that would prevent illness are not used. In fact, preventive medical procedures are not reimbursed by most health care plans.

Several solutions have been proposed. We discuss two here.

One proposal is free market competition. This suggestion is predicated on the basic assumption that the consumer is able and equipped to make intelligent and informed decisions. It assumes that, as with any other product, when providers are forced to compete for consumers' business, they will improve the quality of their services.

Consumer choice is important, but it has a major limitation. It assumes a sufficient level of consumer literacy. According to the National Assessment of Adult Literacy, conducted by the U.S. Department of Education, "Health literacy is the ability to obtain, process, and understand health information and use that information to make appropriate decisions about one's health and medical care."[31] The results on almost twenty thousand American individuals sixteen years and older were completed in 2003. The assessment found that 12 percent of participants had proficient health literacy skills, 22 percent had basic skills, and 14 percent had below basic skills. In other words, ninety million Americans have inadequate health literacy and are not able to reliably obtain, understand, and use health-related information to make appropriate and informed decisions about their health and medical care.[32]

The second proposal is to hand out *health care report cards.* Structural measures, such as the nurse-to-patient ratio in a hospital, and process measures, such as the number of cholesterol tests in a population at risk, are the main components in many report cards. Unfortunately, the direct relationship of structural measures to health outcomes is difficult to determine. Process measures may explain only a small number of patient outcomes; nevertheless, process measures are predominant in report cards.

In collaboration with Dr. Michael DeBakey, widely acclaimed pioneer in coronary artery bypass graft surgery, Silvers produced estimates of thirty-day, five-year, and ten-year survival rates subsequent to surgery.[33] Hospitals use similar methods to produce report cards on their overall performance. This information is important, but the proponents of increased competition in the health care system assume that consumers can interpret this information and use it to make informed choices. This is unlikely. The methodology used by Silvers was based on very sophisticated statistical ideas. Interpretation of the report card, even for the medically literate, is thus a difficult task.

HEALTH CARE POLICY

The so-called free market system drives economic growth, but the dividends are not necessarily well distributed. The government has historically played a major role in distributing the benefits of economic growth and protecting the public from risks to their health and welfare. Economist Robert Kuttner has shown evidence of the positive role of government.[34] For example, President Lincoln was instrumental in passing the Homestead Act, which enabled poor individuals to own farms. President Franklin Roosevelt and President Harry Truman enabled home mortgages. Truman's GI Bill of Rights allowed veterans to have access to higher education and thus to enter into the middle class. The government provides free public education and subsidizes higher education.

The elderly are protected economically by Social Security. The State Children's Health Insurance Program has provided poor children and families with health care support. The public's safety has been improved by the FDA's control of new pharmaceuticals. The Environmental Protection Agency's regulation of toxic substances has sought to protect against reproductive and neurological abnormalities.

However, government policies based on cost cutting can also lead to diminished public protection. For example, in order to try to save money, the government has radically changed the role of the FDA in ensuring the public's safety. In 1992, Congress enacted the Prescription Drug User Fee Act, which required drug companies to pay $576,000 to the FDA for each new drug application, to help pay for the costs of the drug evaluation procedures.[35] Most of the money was intended to speed up drug approvals. Because the emphasis was on getting drugs to market faster, safety became a lesser priority. Since the enactment, "a record 13 prescription drugs have had to be withdrawn from the market after they caused hundreds of deaths."[36]

The imposition of user fees has also led to conflicts of interest; if the fees were removed, the security of many FDA staffers could be jeopardized, because the government would engage in cost containment. Further, the FDA's standing advisory committees for the approval of new drugs consist of many experts who have financial links to the drug companies, contrary to the FDA's policy.

CONCLUDING REMARKS:
THE TYPE FOUR ERRORS OF HEALTH CARE

The Type Four Error of the U.S. health care system can be boiled down to the following quesion: *How can the AMA, the big HMOs, the insurance companies, and other powerful interests solve the problem of getting the public to accept the notion that maximizing profits at the public's expense is the problem worth solving?* In other words, the fundamental Type Four Error has been to focus on getting the public to accept the definitions of the problem as posed by the big corporations, the HMOs, and so on. Their solution? A potent combination of fear tactics, a false ideology and philosophy about the nature of the world (for instance, that the quantity and quality of health care can be separated), sustained propaganda, effective public relations, and distortions. These have been the means of securing the end of huge and obscene profits, literally at the expense of the public's health.

At best, the U.S. system "solves" health problems for those who can afford it. At worst, even those who can afford it find out that the insurance companies are very good at finding ways of denying them what they have already paid for. As a result, the U.S. health care system has become a system for generating huge profits for the big HMOs, insurance providers, and drug companies.

One of the cures that have been proposed for the system is a call for greater competition between different private insurance companies and HMOs. In short, reward those for-profit organizations that deliver better care at a more competitive cost. In other words, more competition will lead to more, that is, to better results for all of us. Although we are certainly not opposed to the private enterprise system or to capitalism in general, we do see a major problem, which we alluded to in Chapter One, that is, the rise of what we refer to as sociopathic capitalism. The present form of health care delivery has so distorted our faith in unfettered capitalism that we are unable to give ourselves over completely to purely private solutions to the problem of health care. In short, we believe the time is right for the government to step in and offer universal health care.

How the government can offer and pay for universal health care is certainly a major problem; nonetheless, it is the "right" problem, on which we should be focusing.

4   NATIONAL INSECURITY
The Failure to Understand
Why Bigger Is No Longer Better

Cemeteries and toxic waste dumps grow each year, but they don't develop.
—RUSSELL ACKOFF[1]

THE WAR IN IRAQ:
THE WORSE OFF WE HAVE BECOME

The more we have spent on the war on terror, the worse off, not the better, we have become. In brief, *more spending has led to less real security*. In even pithier terms, *more has led to less*.

By any and all measures, the war on terror is one of the biggest Type Four Errors in U.S. history. For instance, in terms of economic cost alone, the latest estimates are that by 2017 the Iraq and Afghanistan wars could cost taxpayers $3 trillion.[2]

By now all but the most intransigent, diehard, true believers dispute the truth of the repeated instances of out-and-out lying and deception, the mismanagement, the corruption, and the sheer incompetence on the part of the Bush administration. Indeed, studies have confirmed that President Bush and top officials of his administration not only lied repeatedly but did so hundreds of times in order to goad the public into going to war under false pretenses. As bad as these actions were—and make no mistake about it, they were very bad—the real failure and tragedy of the Bush administration was its fundamental inability and unwillingness to come to grips with the fact that both war and the world have changed profoundly since 1945 and the advent of technologies such as the atomic bomb and mass communications that are global in their reach. Thus, the abject failures, multiple fiascos, and tragedies of the Bush administration, including the more obvious failures such as the poor response to Katrina, were far worse and much deeper than have previously been analyzed. To be fair, however, we are not sure that the Democrats, despite all their rhetoric, really understand what's truly different about today's world. In short, the logic or rules of the systems age are very different from those of the machine age, that is, the long-gone world of the industrial revolution.

To understand more fully the flawed reasoning and choices of the Bush administration, we turn to an examination of the so-called logic underlying the Cold War. Doing this will allow us to see that the same kinds of flawed reasoning have been a major feature of democratic as well as republican administrations.

1984

In 1984, Mitroff performed one of the first analyses of the full set of paradoxes associated with nuclear weapons.[3] To date it is still one of the few analyses to do so.[4] It turns out there is not a single issue related to nuclear weapons that is not subject to paradox.

Up to 1984, most analysts were aware of, and hence concentrated their efforts on dealing with, a single, central paradox: because both sides—the party that initiated it as well the party that responded in kind—would lose equally in a nuclear war, *nuclear weapons existed for the purpose of not being used.* It was finally realized that in a nuclear war there would be no winners, only losers. Nuclear weapons could not actually be used. Their primary power lay in deterring their use and thus in preventing a nuclear war. This realization was enshrined in the doctrine of *mutual assured destruction,* or MAD for short—an appropriate acronym if ever there was one! If one followed the argument through to its logically illogical conclusion, then MAD said something like this: The two superpowers of the time, the Soviets and the United States, could each destroy the other so many times over that it didn't matter which one struck first. The survivor would still have enough nuclear firepower remaining to inflict fatal damage on the initiator of a nuclear war. Because the situation was completely symmetrical, both sides realized that it was prudent *not* to use their immense nuclear arsenals against each other.

Although MAD worked in the sense that it ensured a standoff, it still created a deep sense of existential dread because, if it failed, Armageddon was inevitable. But then the foreboding sense of Armageddon was itself part of the entire train of thought behind MAD. MAD not only fueled itself but was also its own rationale and justification.

An even more radical conclusion emerged. Because our knowledge of the atom could not be uninvented, nuclear weapons could not be uninvented either. Therefore, the notion of nuclear weapons had to be rethought entirely. It was finally realized that they had to be reconceptualized as nuclear "devices." This was anything but a clever play on words. Reclassifying weapons as devices meant they could no longer be thought of as weapons. This may seem like semantics alone, but it actually had deep implications for pragmatics, that is, for actions and policies.

Unfortunately, the paradoxes were just beginning; MAD did not exhaust them by any means. Reclassifying and renaming nuclear weapons as nuclear devices did not eliminate their threat. In the following paragraphs we further demonstrate the paradoxes posed by complex issues such as nuclear weapons.

More Leads to More

The simplest way to understand how and why the whole phenomenon of nuclear weapons was, and still is, chock full of paradoxes is as follows: Suppose one has a missile buried deep in the ground in a silo in order to protect it from an enemy attack. To protect the missile even further, it makes sense to "harden" the silo by pouring lots of reinforced concrete on top of it. The thinking is that this will make it even harder for enemy missiles to penetrate and destroy our missiles. The chain of reasoning behind this idea is captured succinctly in the notion that *more of something good*—in this case, more protection conferred by more concrete—*leads to more of another good that one is trying to achieve*, that is, greater felt security and peace of mind. In pithier terms: *more leads to more.*

More Leads to Less

Unfortunately, pouring more concrete on top of our silos only encouraged the Soviets to put more nuclear warheads on top of their "bad-guy" missiles, to increase their firepower so they could more easily penetrate our "good-guy" silos. The result was that more of something that was initially felt to be good—more reinforced concrete on top of our silos—actually led to less felt security. So, hardening our silos only fueled the arms race instead of lessening it. In this sense, it had the complete opposite of the intended effect.

Less Leads to More

It therefore made sense to consider putting less concrete on top of silos. The reasoning here was that *less leads to more.* That is, less concrete signals that we wish to be less of a threat to the enemy; or although we obviously intend to threaten them, we only want to do so in order to deter them. We don't want to threaten them so much that we frighten and thus provoke them into initiating a first-strike, preemptive nuclear war.

Of course this approach assumed not only that the enemy *could* distinguish between what we meant by offensive weapons and what we meant by defensive weapons, but also that they *wanted* to distinguish between them as we did (and of course it assumed that we wanted to distinguish between them as well). It also assumed that the distinction between offensive and defensive nuclear weapons or devices is valid. Unfortunately, because of the enormous destructive potential of nuclear weapons, the distinction collapsed. Anything that protected nuclear weapons was viewed as offensive as well as defensive.

Less Leads to Less
Less leads to less, however, is also a real possibility. Less concrete can lead to less felt security. After all, one's missiles are then more exposed and therefore more vulnerable to attack. The attitude that less leads to less can be interpreted as a sign of weakness, and therefore that we have lost our basic will and resolve to fight.

AN ENDLESS LOOP
It slowly began to dawn on the strategic war analysts in the United States and the old Soviet Union that we were both caught in an endless loop. Because trust was lacking on both sides, there was no way of stopping the dynamics of the situation once it was started. *Engaging just one element of the chain of reasoning, such as more leads to more, inevitably led to all of the other elements.*

The only thing that could stop the cycle, the game, altogether was complete and reliable trust. But if there were complete and reliable trust, the whole nuclear arms race wouldn't have gotten started in the first place! Henry Kissinger once said that if a nuclear war started between the United States and the Soviet Union, then both sides would have to behave with extreme caution, restraint, and rationality to keep it from getting out of hand. What Kissinger never explained is that if extreme caution, restraint, and rationality were lacking *before* a war broke out and thus had not kept it from happening in the first place, how would they magically appear *in* the heat of battle, when mental and emotional faculties are strained to the point of breaking? So much for brilliant thinkers!

THE MANAGEMENT OF PARADOX
Because of their very nature as immensely terrifying and destructive powers, and because of the enormous uncertainties surrounding their use, *the phenomenon of nuclear weapons fits simultaneously in all four of the preceding categories of paradox* (more leads to

more, more leads to less, less leads to more, and less leads to less). *The management of nuclear weapons is thus precisely the management of paradox.*

Another complication, and one that is still not fully appreciated, is that the definitions of *more* and *less* cannot be standardized. What's more and what's less invariably depends on who is looking at the situation. Our definition of what's more is not the same as the enemy's. In other words, the inherent lack of clarity regarding the definitions of *more* and *less* is a major characteristic of the whole phenomenon of nuclear weapons.

Unfortunately, all of the paradoxes and ambiguities inherent in nuclear weapons have never been realized and learned completely by the politicians and policy analysts, let alone by the general public. We therefore have not yet learned that the nature of warfare has changed dramatically since the invention and first use of the atomic bomb in 1945. Lack of clarity and precision is not only a prime characteristic of the use of nuclear weapons but also an essential characteristic of modern warfare. For example, how does one completely and reliably differentiate between insurgents and friendly populations when they are virtually indistinguishable? This is especially true of terrorism. Terrorists don't wear uniforms to identify themselves and don't reveal their locations. Fuzziness, or the lack of complete clarity regarding the key concepts and attributes of terrorism, is one of the key elements of terrorism! In other words, the definition of terrorism is part of the "mess" that is terrorism.

Another deeply troubling fact is that the same considerations that apply to every aspect of nuclear weapons also apply to every aspect of modern warfare. For instance, consider the role of uncertainty. Uncertainty on the part of the enemy regarding what we would actually do in a nuclear confrontation would supposedly lead to caution on the enemy's part and thus lead to greater security for us. The assumption, in short, is that greater uncertainty leads to greater security. A moment's reflection, however, is enough to show that more uncertainty *could* provoke the enemy and hence lead to less felt security.

Unfortunately, these dynamics of the role of uncertainty are being played out in Iraq and elsewhere with respect to torture. For example, if the enemy knows for sure that the United States regards waterboarding as torture and hence will definitively not use it, they will not—at least so goes the argument—be deterred from attacking us because we will have given away our strategic advantage by tipping our hand. The less the enemy knows about what we will and will not do, then the more, supposedly, they will be deterred.

(As an important aside, in waterboarding a damp cloth is placed over the mouth and nose of a person and then water is constantly dripped over the cloth. The effect is akin to the feeling that one is drowning even though one is not. To be clear, we are completely and utterly opposed to such practices. We are repulsed merely by describing it.)

TRADITIONAL THINKING

The idea that more leads to more is one of the key defining elements of traditional warfare. Five hundred years ago, if we had an army of ten thousand men and you had an army of only a thousand men, and they all used traditional weapons such as bows and arrows, our army would generally be superior to yours. If the idea that *more leads to more*, or *bigger is better*, applied to our army, then *less leads to less* applied to yours. *Weakness leads only to further weakness.* Nuclear weapons changed all of this. If you have only fifty nuclear warheads and we have a hundred, the difference doesn't matter if fifteen are enough to blow each side to kingdom come. Unfortunately, because there are still so many nuclear weapons, the situation continues to be as precarious.

The situation was made even worse by the fact that both sides could place their warheads on nuclear submarines—which indeed they could during the Cold War—and thus hide them in the vast oceans of the world. Doing so made it even more likely that whoever survived an initial attack would have more than enough firepower to destroy the other side umpteen times over.

The traditional logic of warfare that had been the order for millennia broke down completely, and forever.

PUZZLES VERSUS MYSTERIES

Writing in the June 2007 issue of *Smithsonian Magazine*, George F. Treverton, director of the RAND Corporation's Center for Global Risk and Security and former vice chairman of the National Intelligence Council, captured the situation we are describing as follows:

Puzzles can be solved; they have *answers*. [Puzzles are thus the same as exercises as described in Chapter Two.] But a mystery offers no such comfort. [A mystery is equivalent to ill-structured problems, if not wicked problems.] It poses a question that has no definitive answer because the answer is contingent; it depends on a future interaction of many factors, known and unknown.

During the cold war, much of the job of U.S. intelligence was puzzle-solving—seeking answers to questions that had answers, even if we didn't know them. How many missiles did the Soviet Union have? Where were they located? How far could they travel? How accurate were they? [In other words, answers could be sought because the questions could be posed in the first place.] It made sense to approach the military strength of the Soviet Union as a puzzle—the sum of its units and weapons, and their quality. But the collapse of the Soviet Union and the rise of terrorism changed all that. Those events upended U.S. intelligence, to the point that *its major challenge is to frame mysteries.* . . . [That is, the major challenge is to define the questions.]

To analysts in the Pentagon . . . terrorists present the ultimate asymmetric threat. *But the nature of the threat is a mystery, not a puzzle.* Terrorists shape themselves to our vulnerabilities, to the seams in our defenses; the threat they pose depends on us. . . . [5]

In other words, politicians and generals are not only constantly fighting the last wars, but they are constantly trying to solve the last puzzles of the last, or the most recent, wars as well. From the standpoint of national security, building an antimissile shield is a prime example of solving the wrong problem precisely because there are serious doubts that any antimissile shield could ever work perfectly, and building one would only encourage the arms race. (Even if only one missile got through, it would wreak enormous damage.) Of course, from the standpoint of its proponents, an antimissile shield is a prime example of *more leads to more*. Therefore, it is considered good. From the standpoint of its opponents, however, it is a prime example of *more leads to less*. At best, then, it is an enormous waste of money and resources. At worst, it is the height of folly and delusion.

Also note that from the standpoint of the military-industrial complex and its supporters, building an antimissile shield is the "right solution" to the problem of "staying in power by means of controlling enormous budgets."[6] Once again, what's "right" and what's "wrong" cannot be decoupled from one's values, belief system, and general view of the world.

The situation is even more complicated than Treverton has stated, however. The "problem" of terrorism is more than a mystery. It is a "wicked" problem. Recall from Chapter Two that wicked problems are those that resist formulation by any and all known academic disciplines and professions. We can't even define wicked problems, let alone solve them; but because we can't ignore them altogether, we have no choice but to deal with them in some way. After all, ignoring them presupposes that we know enough about them—and thus have defined them to a certain extent—to safely ignore (and thus resolve or dissolve) them. As we noted in Chapter Two, wicked problems are "coped with" but never fully solved.

THE BIGGEST ERROR

One conclusion emerges from our discussion thus far. The biggest error of most contemporary presidential administrations, not just of the Bush administration, has been to think that the so-called war on terror is a puzzle to be solved and therefore can be fought and won as such. Although the initial invasion of Iraq and the defeat of Saddam Hussein's army may have been rightly conceptualized and fought as puzzles, the subsequent insurgency has not been.

The result of treating this mystery as a puzzle is as follows: The more we have spent on the war on terror, the worse off we have become. In short, more has led to less. The war on terror and doing more and more of the same to fight it is one of the biggest Type Four Errors in U.S. history.

So was the creation of the Department of Homeland Security. Putting separate dysfunctional organizations such as the Office of Intelligence and Analysis, the Federal Emergency Management Agency, and so on into one big dysfunctional organization is another prime example of solving the wrong problem. It has merely created a super-dysfunctional agency.

The trick is to create new forms of organization that can compete with the enemy's organizations, such as Al Qaeda, but that obviously are not evil themselves in their intent or actions. Such organizations need to be highly flexible, adaptive, and decentralized, not old-time rigid bureaucracies. Once again, less is more.

OTHER INTERPRETATIONS

In addition to the usual interpretation that bigger is better, the expression *more leads to more* can also be interpreted as "stay the course," "if at first you don't succeed, then do more of the same," or as Senator John McCain has put it, "success breeds success."

On the other hand, the expression *more leads to less* can be interpreted as "it isn't working anymore," "bigness only gets in the way; the new success is doing more with less," "mean and lean beats out big and tired every time," "the world is sending us a strong signal that it's time to change," or "we have reached a tipping point." The phrase *less is more* recognizes not only that one needs to change, but also that one is willing and ready to embark on the journey toward that change.

The expression *less leads to less* recognizes that the time for significant and meaningful change may have passed by: "it's too little too late," "we're in a state of inevitable decline," and as Senator John McCain has put it, "failure breeds failure."

More leads to more and *less leads to more* can be interpreted as best-case scenarios, while *less leads to less* and *more leads to less* can be understood as worst-case scenarios at this point in our quest for national security. Thus, depending on which scenario they are looking at, and on whether they are applying it to business or to government, both liberals and conservatives can be either best-case optimists or worst-case pessimists.

THE TYPE FOUR ERRORS
OF THE BUSH ADMINISTRATION

We are finally in a position to look at the Type Four Errors of the Bush administration as they pertain to the Iraq war. Through the continual use of fear, lies, deception, and a narrow point of view and ideology, the Bush administration continually sold the propositions *more leads to more* and *less leads to less* as the only two options open to us. By ignoring the other two propositions—*more leads to less* and *less leads to more*—it committed an incalculable Type Four Error: *it repeatedly solved the wrong problem by not solving the whole problem.* One might wish to argue that this was a Type Three Error because *more leads to more* is a tactic of traditional warfare. An optimist might say that the Bush administration made this error simply by accident, by following the precedents of the past. However, this error was unmistakably Type Four because it disregarded signs that the "old hat" didn't fit anyone. Intention was the key difference.

One can also see the catastrophic consequences of this kind of Type Four Error—not solving the whole problem—in any effort to extricate us from Iraq. Any proposal for removing U.S. troops runs quickly into all four propositions. Every proposal has good and bad consequences simultaneously. Even worse, every proposal cycles through every proposition so fast that it is difficult to differentiate what's good from what's bad. One begins to see why the problems of the nuclear and global information age can only be called "wicked."

Something even more fundamental emerges as well from examining the flawed approach of the Bush administration. In the nuclear age and the age of terrorism, it is not clear that wars can still be won in the conventional sense of the term. More than we realize, modern warfare owes more to the field of health care than we can begin to imagine. Terrorism is like a serious and incurable virus, and as such it can only be "managed," never fully eliminated or eradicated.

The perpetrators of modern warfare also need to realize that, like health, true security depends more on the *quality* of security than on the sheer *quantity* of it. Also, because of the global economy and the extreme interconnectedness of the world, it is completely false to say that if we don't fight them over there, we will have to fight them here. There are no distinct "theres" and "heres" anymore. The fight is literally everywhere at once.

We are also finally in a position to begin to see how and why individuals, organizations, institutions, and even whole societies get trapped into *repeatedly* committing Type Four Errors. Essentially they cannot break free from the chain of reasoning from *bigger is better* to *stay the course* to *when in trouble, do more of the same.* Conversely, those who not only survive but prosper in a complex and turbulent world realize that different times require fundamentally different modes of thinking and behaving. They realize that there are no alternatives to change, that is, to doing more and better with less.

MORE LEADS TO MORE IN OUR HISTORY

The paradoxes of today, such as that more leads to more, reach far back to and have been with us since the beginnings of our existence as a nation. Those who founded America had fled the repressive, centralized regimes of Europe. As a result, they had a deep and abiding distrust of all big, centralized powers. For this reason alone they deliberately created a weak federal government. However, this move had a huge, unintended consequence: a weak federal government proved ultimately to be unable to prevent the rise of another form of huge, centralized power: private corporations, or big business.

The original intention of course was that *greater controls on the size of government would lead to greater freedom from tyranny.* That is, less (smaller, weaker) government would lead to (ensure) more freedom. In short, the reasoning was that less would lead to more. Instead, what resulted was less led to less.

This is not just another example of less leading to less. It is part of a primal condition or fault line that haunts America to this day. Because this concept is so important to understand, we want to quote at length from Charles Perrow, who has made the point eloquently:

How did it come about that the United States developed an economic system based upon large corporations, privately held, with minimal regulation by the state? Two hundred years ago there were none. Until the 1890s there were only a few large ones, in textiles and railroads and the steel and locomotive industries. Then there was a spurt at the turn of the century; in about 5 years most of the 200 biggest corporations of the time were formed, and most of these still rule their industries.

Nothing comparable occurred in Europe. Until the 1950s the corporate structure of the United States was unique, and it was dominant in the industrialized world. Some of the reasons for this American "exceptionalism" are familiar: The industrial revolution found fertile ground in a resource-rich land with mass markets and democratic institutions in a culture of individual freedom and entrepreneurship. But two things have not been emphasized enough: In the United States, a weak state did not prevent large concentrations of economic power and did not provide strong state regulation, in contrast to Europe's stronger states. Second, concentrated power with large-scale production was also possible for organizational reasons: Organizations changed the legal system to give organizations sovereignty, and they had a wage-dependent population that permitted a bureaucratic structure with tight labor control.

For large corporations to spring into existence at the end of the century, the legal structure of the commonwealth had to be reworked. It had to favor the accumulation of private capital for large-scale production for national markets, rather [than] the dispersion of capital into small enterprises with regional markets. It appears that the United States centralized private wealth and power a century sooner than Europe did. *Our global success then forced our solution upon Europe in the last half of the twentieth century.*

The weak state and the organizational arguments are interdependent. Assuming a minimal degree of democracy, we can argue that (a) [a] weak state will allow private organizations to grow almost without limit and with few requirements to serve the public interests; and (b) private organizations will shape the weak state to its liking (this requires state action, in the form of changing property laws). A strong state, however, would have sufficient legislative independence of private economic organizations, and sufficient executive strength and will to check the power of private organizations. Together these could limit their growth and require some attention to the public interest. This happened to a greater degree in Europe than in the United States.[7]

The key role of the railroads in organizing America was possible because they passed, quite quickly, into private hands with no significant regulation in the public interest. We were the only nation to allow the privatization of this immense public good. . . . the most fierce strikes of the [1800s] . . . concerned railroads. Their labor policies set the antagonistic tone for all future capital-labor relations. And their bureaucratic control structure, so celebrated in organizational theory, became the model for both public and private organizations. *Bureaucracy has proved to be the best unobtrusive control device ever invented by elites.*[8]

Of course hindsight is twenty-twenty. We shouldn't blame our forefathers for not foreseeing all the consequences of their thoughts and actions.

THINGS MAY HAVE GOTTEN WORSE

Since the demise of the former Soviet Union, things may have gotten even worse. Nuclear "devices" may have once again become "weapons," thus demonstrating that the labels we give to problems are never fixed. Unlike exercises and puzzles, which once solved stay solved, problems have to be continually "managed":

- Nine countries can now deliver nuclear warheads on ballistic missiles, and Iran wants to join this club. Several nations could hit targets anywhere in the world, but regional salvos might be more likely.

- Today's weapons would exact greater death and injury than the bomb dropped on Hiroshima. . . .

- The U.S. has embarked on a 25-year program to replace thousands of aging . . . nuclear warheads, which military officials say could be degrading. Proponents claim that the substitute weapon—the Reliable Replacement Warhead (RRW)—is essential to maintaining the U.S. stockpile as a credible deterrent. [That is, newer is better, or leads to more.] Critics argue that the RRW is a waste of billions of dollars and could goad other nations into a renewed nuclear arms race. [That is, newer is not necessarily better, and does not necessarily lead to more.][9]

Never underestimate the military-industrial complex's willingness to sell us the proposition that more is better.

Writing in *The Nation*, nuclear abolitionist Jonathan Schell put it as follows:

The new era has brought a new set of nuclear dangers to the fore. In the cold war, the most salient lesson was that the bomb is equally destructive to all; in the post-cold war era, the inescapable lesson is that the bomb's technology is equally available to all competent producers, very likely including, one day not far off, terrorist groups. In the cold war, the driving force was the bilateral arms race; in the post-cold war era, it has been proliferation.[10]

It should be clear that conservatives generally favor *bigger is better* when it comes to private enterprise but *smaller is better* or *less is more* when it comes to government. The exception is of course the military. There, bigger is better.

Above all, conservatives wouldn't be caught dead with *less leads to less*, because they fundamentally believe that *less is dead*. It is the exact opposite for liberals. Big government, except for the military, is good while big business is inherently bad. It's a shame that conservatives and liberals have such differing views of the military, because strangely enough the military has much to teach us about the size of organizations in a global economy. It is not an accident of history that the size of an army battalion is four hundred soldiers.[11] Above four hundred, people can no longer recognize one another by sight and relate to one another on a first-name basis. They have to rely on abstractions such as "he/she works for the XYZ division over in building 40128C."

There is a key lesson in this for organizations, both public and private. For organizations to grow they need to find ways to group themselves into units no bigger than four hundred people. In other words, organizations should not confuse growth with development.

As Russell Ackoff has said many times, "Cemeteries and toxic waste dumps grow each year, but they don't develop!"[12]

In the end, there is no final answer to the question, *What is the optimal size of an organization?* This question is a problem, not a puzzle. The answer depends on one's purposes. Yet the question is equivalent to the ancient, and silly, puzzle, *If we keep adding small grains of sand to a small pile, when does it become a heap?* No one can give a complete answer to such a question independent of the contexts and consequences in which it can occur. Indeed, problems have contexts, puzzles do not. The point is that we have a prime instance of a puzzle (an exercise) that cannot be solved in principle, whereas if it were converted into a problem, it potentially could be solved, or at least managed.

THE GLOBAL ECONOMY

The four paradoxes we have considered in relation to nuclear weapons have direct parallels in the new global economy. By virtue of its extreme interconnectedness and because of the ability of businesses to conduct their affairs at the speed of light, the global economy obeys the propositions that more leads to more, more leads to less, and so on. In fact, it obeys all of them at once.

The economies of the world are now so intertwined that in effect we have created the financial equivalent of MAD, as the recent volatility of the U.S. stock market and the subprime credit crisis demonstrate. A serious recession, or its threat, in one economy creates a serious threat in all others. A mortgage crisis in one economy quickly spreads to mortgage crises in others.

Up until the 1980s, bigger was unquestionably and unequivocally better. Big organizations literally ran the world. Consider General Motors (GM), the quintessential example of bigness. When we think of organizations like GM, the notion that most readily comes to mind is *economies of scale*. Because of their ability to control the distribution of their products, the costs of labor and materials, and so on, big organizations, like GM, were once able to lower significantly the costs of producing products for a mass audience. They were also able, by means of huge advertising budgets, to shape what consumers want. They could easily get large groups of consumers to want the same things. As a result, they were able to corner their markets.

In the case of GM, consumers were offered and accepted a limited number of choices when it came to cars, which made it much, much easier for GM to plan what to make and how to make it. Through the creation of mass markets and consumption, it could control manufacturing costs.

As Robert Reich and many others have pointed out, things began to change noticeably around the 1990s, if not long before. Indeed, dramatic changes were afoot in the 1960s and 1970s because the Japanese and the other "Asian tigers" were altering the ways in which they conducted business.

The Internet has only amplified and speeded up such changes. Along with effecting fundamental changes in manufacturing practices and in the nature of organizations, the Internet has made bigness no longer a distinct and decisive advantage. Small suppliers and manufacturers can challenge and take on the big guys. Not only can the small guys more easily adapt to local market conditions (because they are more responsive and nimble), but via the Internet they can also coordinate the manufacturing and distribution of goods across the entire globe. They can contract with anyone they wish—even the big guys—who is willing to make what they want, when and where they want it, and at the cheapest prices available. In other words, more of a better technology—in this case, the Internet—has led to smaller (that is, less) being better. In some cases, small is even "beautiful," that is, it has led to businesses being "green" by reducing waste.

A few organizations, such as Wal-Mart, have even learned how to be both big and small at the same time, and hence have learned how to reap the benefits of both. By virtue of its size—and thus its immense bargaining power—Wal-Mart can scan the globe to find those companies that are willing to manufacture items to its specs and at the cheapest prices to be found anywhere. It then passes on the savings directly to its customers. To accomplish this, Wal-Mart uses the Internet and the latest information technologies to its advantage, to coordinate its dealings with thousands of manufacturers and suppliers worldwide. It uses computers to read barcodes so that it can keep track almost instantly of what items are being sold where and when. It can thus determine what to buy and what to distribute. This approach has made Wal-Mart extremely responsive to the needs of its customers.

Of course not everyone agrees with Wal-Mart's practices, especially with how it mistreats its employees. We certainly don't.

CONCLUDING REMARKS

In this chapter we have primarily considered modern warfare as an illustration of where the notion that bigger is better breaks down and more leads to less. This breakdown occurs when the situations in which we intervene are so complex that bigness turns back on itself and unintentionally becomes the enemy.

To recap, it is true that bigger armies are traditionally better (that is, stronger) than smaller ones, but this does not mean they can increase in size indefinitely. Bigger armies are also harder to feed, clothe, supply, and transport than smaller ones. Somewhere along the line, size becomes a "tipping point," and if anything is a prime indicator that we are solving the wrong problems precisely, then surely it is the existence of tipping points.

This chapter has also shown that the management of paradoxes is at the heart of global phenomena. In Chapter Seven we show in detail how paradoxes can be managed. In particular, we show how Errors of the Third and Fourth Kinds can actually be assessed, and hopefully without committing further errors. The last thing we wish to do is commit Errors of the Third and Fourth Kinds while assessing Errors of the Third and Fourth Kinds!

5

THE MEDIA

Reinventing Reality

JFK Reloaded, a Scottish firm, launched the so-called docugame on the anniversary of the assassination last week. The game's website (jfk-reloaded .com) is offering up to $*100,000* to the player who most closely re-creates the shots Lee Harvey Oswald fired. . . . (Points are subtracted for hitting Jackie.) . . . the site has received more than *500,000* hits.[1]

THE PHENOMENON OF UNREALITY

In this chapter we discuss the general concept of *unreality* and the various forms it assumes in everyday life. We also discuss the major mechanisms that are responsible for the creation and dissemination of unreality. As we show, these mechanisms are also examples of very clever and subtle forms of Type Four Errors.

We analyze unreality primarily through how it affects and is affected by the media. Although unreality pervades every nook and cranny of modern life, it is most readily seen in the media. By focusing on the media we show how unreality shapes the definition of important problems, thereby leading to important forms of Type Three and Type Four Errors.

A SENSE OF UNREALITY: A TENTATIVE DEFINITION

In everyday speech, the word *unreality* is used in several ways. Each of these ways conveys an important meaning of the term. Unreality, then, variously means:

1. A person, an object, or a scene of nature that is so unusually beautiful, striking, surreal, and so on that ordinary reality pales in comparison: "She's so beautiful, it's unreal"; "You had to be there to believe it; the whole scene was unreal."

2. A computer-generated reality that looks so much like the "real thing" that it cannot be easily differentiated from it: "It looked so real I couldn't tell whether it was or not; in fact, it was more real than reality." Increasingly we not only have the ability to generate computer-produced images that look like the real thing, but we can also interject these images seamlessly into "reality." Indeed, they are the "new reality."

3. An act of evil that is incomprehensible to the ordinary person: "How could anyone even think of, let alone do, such terrible things [such as Nazi Germany or Bosnia]?"

4. A computer-generated game that violates ordinary physical laws: "Objects in this game don't obey the laws of gravity and motion."

5. An argument or action that is so egregious that it offends ordinary moral standards: "How could anyone say, let alone justify, such things?" (Recall the discussion of Don Imus in Chapter One.)

6. A dangerous or odd situation in which a person finds himself or herself and exclaims spontaneously, "I can't believe this is happening to me; it's completely unreal."

7. The deliberate use of a myth, such as an idealized version of small-town America that has only ever existed in our dreams and imaginations.

8. A public act that once would have been shocking and unthinkable, such as the wanton and revealing displays of young women and men in provocative poses on Web sites such as Facebook.

9. The deliberate, nonstop manufacturing of celebrities and pseudo-celebrities that feeds our constant need for fantasies and characters (victims, villains, heroes, and so on) who are larger than life in order to blunt the harshness of everyday life.

10. The constant use of deception, lies, and fear mongering to sell unpopular ideas, such as the Iraq war.

Unreality is all of these things and more.

One of the most distinctive features of unreality is that all of the types just listed are strongly interdependent. In effect, each form of unreality is intertwined with all of the other forms. Nonetheless, in this chapter we focus primarily on forms two, four, seven, eight, nine, and ten. They lead to the following tentative and working definition of unreality: *Unreality is the deliberate creation and use of arguments, images, myths, and tactics that not only distort, enhance, and replace ordinary reality but also attempt to convince us that unreality is better than reality.* Thus, unreality is the solution to the problem of how to replace and remanufacture reality. It is in this way that unreality is a Type Four Error.

For example, although we further discuss the idealized myth and fantasy of small-town America in a moment, consider how it predisposes us to view health care. If we accept the myth, it leads us to the conclusion that there is no need for universal health care because in small-town America everyone basically looks out for and takes care of everyone else. Thus there is no need for government involvement— period! Besides, it is the basic responsibility of individuals and not the government to solve our problems. Furthermore, all problems are basically and essentially individual. After all, in the idealized fantasy version of America, institutionalized problems such as racism don't exist. All problems are due to individuals who presumably can work things out by themselves. In this way, the issue of health care, which we discussed in Chapter Three, and unreality are related.

As another brief example, consider that the media have all but abandoned their fundamental role of reporting reality. They are more interested in the invention and dissemination of unreality (witness the constant creation and consumption of pseudo-celebrities) than in serving as a check on powerful individuals, institutions, and special interest groups who define reality to serve their own purposes instead of those of the wider public. In this way the production and consumption of unreality is one of the biggest Type Four Errors, because it contributes to the skewing of information about situations in which decisions must be made.

THE PERVASIVENESS OF UNREALITY

Although the existence and operation of unreality are seen most clearly in the media, especially TV, unreality is pervasive. It is an integral part of how we decide life and death issues, such as whether to go or not go to war, whether weapons of mass destruction exist, whether to vote or not vote for a particular candidate, or even whether to vote at all. Unreality is also found in the choices we make about where to live and how we look.

One of the most important aspects of unreality is the determination of who and what humans will be in the not-so-distant future. The ultimate unreality project is the redesigning and remanufacturing of humans. We are on the verge of nothing less than the transformation (transmutation?) of humans into cyborgs—ungodly mixtures of human and machine—via organ regeneration and replacement, chip implants, enhancements, and so on.

Because unreality is so pervasive, the simpleminded admonition to "just turn off the TV" is meaningless. Although one can still turn off a TV set, one can't turn off an entire culture. We certainly can't turn off a TV-saturated culture in which newspapers such as *USA Today* are modeled directly after a TV screen. It's even harder to turn off a constantly connected culture in which Facebook and YouTube are primary means of creating our social reality, identity, and selfhood. Descartes' famous proposition "I think, therefore I am" has been replaced with "I connect constantly; therefore I am only in the eyes of others."

This is not to say that the media, and TV in particular, are all bad. As many historians and political analysts have pointed out, one of the great redeeming features of TV is that it allows voters to focus, literally, on the tics and mannerisms of candidates.[2] TV reveals character as no other medium does. At the same time, there is little question that TV has dramatically shortened our attention spans. Whereas voters once traveled long distances to hear the Lincoln-Douglas debates, which lasted for more than three hours, we are lucky if we can tolerate more than thirty seconds of uninterrupted sound and TV bites.

A final caveat: as important as it is, we do not discuss media consolidation—the fact that media companies are merging at an alarming rate—and what this portends for news and entertainment. Make no mistake about it: the fact that media companies can now own everything from newspapers to book publishing companies, TV stations, and movie studios has potentially enormous and damaging consequences for what supposedly informed citizens can know. The only reason we don't discuss this is that we are focusing on a more insidious and less visible problem: the creation of unreality on a scale without parallel in human history.

CELEBRATION, FLORIDA:
A DELIBERATELY CONSTRUCTED UNREAL WORLD

To see how deeply embedded unreality is in everyday life, consider the example of a deliberately constructed place where a version of the American dream appears to thrive. It is a snug, quiet, community-centered town where a tasteful blend of stately Victorian, classic Mediterranean, and cozy Colonial homes reign over tree-lined avenues leading to a quaint town center. Residents can stroll to the Lollipop Cottage to buy a pair of child's overalls, or find antique reproductions at Nottingham's. Enthusiasts can play year-round golf or jog safely along miles of wooded paths. And from November 25 through December 31 it snows nightly on Market Street at 6, 7, 8, and 9 P.M.

This isn't Disney World, although a division of Disney developed it. It's not even a theme park. It is a real town where presumably real people live, eat, work, go to school, watch television, and have sex. The town is Celebration, and it literally lies next to Disney's World Resort in Orlando, Florida.

You may have heard of Celebration; it has received a lot of press as one of several "New Urban" planned communities cropping up around the country. You may have scoffed at the idea of people insulating themselves in an artificial, pristine, and sterile universe, where the aesthetics and values are permanently frozen in a white, small-town middle America that historians point out never really existed except in our nostalgia-hungry imaginations. Your cynicism may have gone off the scale when you learned that behind its carefully constructed facade, high-tech gadgets are wired into every home, nook, and cranny, and that for all its pretensions to duplicate small-town America, big retail chains are well represented in Celebration. Finally, you may even have congratulated yourself with the comforting thought that you at least keep your feet firmly on the ground, anchored in reality. The unfortunate truth, though, is that none of us lives in the real world any longer. In fact, we haven't lived in it for some time.

Like visitors to Disney World, the residents of Celebration have consciously chosen to leave the old, real America behind and barricade themselves behind white picket fences. The rest of America, however, lives in an equally artificial world. It may in fact be worse off because it doesn't know it. If we have not already lost it entirely, then we are quickly losing the fundamental ability to differentiate between what's real and what's unreal. Even the most farsighted prognosticators could not have anticipated that not only would we allow unreality to displace reality but we would become enslaved to it. In short, "America the Delusional" is a fitting label for our times. If any doubts remain, then reading Frank Rich's highly disturbing and chilling account of how the Bush administration deliberately sold the Iraq war (amply aided and abetted by the complicity and repeated failures of Congress and the news media) is enough to dispel them.[3]

IT'S NOT NICE TO ANGER OPRAH,
BUT IT MAKES FOR GOOD TV RATINGS

Consider another example: the debacle that occurred some three years ago over a memoir that, as it turns out, wasn't really a memoir at all. James Frey's *Million Little Pieces*, praised as "the *War and*

Peace of addiction," was already a bestseller when Oprah selected it for her book club.[4] As we all know, it was exposed to be at best an embellished account of the author's recovery from addiction, and at worst a complete fabrication. Frey's dishonesty in pursuit of bestsellerdom is a striking example of a major form of unreality: the shameless blurring of the once sacrosanct boundary between truth and out-and-out fiction. To put it mildly, this case puts an interesting twist on the distinctions, if any, between disinformation, misinformation, and information in the "systems age." Indeed, what are the differences between them when the boundaries between truth and fiction have become blurred almost beyond recognition? (As an important aside, this case also reveals our complicity in the blurring of boundaries that were once sacrosanct.) Although *New York Times* writer Thomas Friedman doesn't use the term, *boundary warping* is a prime feature of the new "flat world" of global business that Friedman describes. It may in fact be its prime feature.[5]

As a society, we have learned quite well how to solve the problem of how to blur any and all boundaries. Thus unreality is now a prominent feature of global business, because it is a prominent feature of every aspect of modern life. Indeed, the unwillingness (inability?) of the finance industry to police itself by setting clear boundaries between "legitimate" and "illegitimate" risk is one of the biggest factors responsible for the current financial crisis. In this sense, boundary blurring is a prime example of Type Three and Type Four Errors.

It is one thing to say that all problems are naturally blurred together because they are part of a larger mess (thus Type Three Errors occur when we wrongly attempt to analyze and solve problems independently of the mess in which they exist), but it is quite another thing when we deliberately blur news and entertainment, or reality and unreality, for the purpose of increasing TV ratings—a Type Four Error. Whereas the first kind of blurring is due to the complexity of modern life, the second kind, the deliberate blurring of news and entertainment, does not help us to deal better with messes. Instead, it diverts us from dealing with the problems of a complex world.

Frey attempted to justify his behavior with the paltry excuse that everything in a memoir doesn't have to be literally true. Again, considering how willing we are as a society to accept the blurring of the boundary between reality and unreality, why doesn't his argument fly? Critics and readers didn't question the veracity of Frey's story precisely because it was such a good story. Even if a few details made us suspicious, it made us feel good to believe it. It's no coincidence that the American Dialect Society voted for *truthiness* as its 2005 Word of the Year. Coined by comedian Stephen Colbert, the word is defined as "the quality of preferring concepts or facts one wishes to be true, rather than concepts or facts known to be true."[6] (The quality that this word identifies is one of the more interesting forms of Type Three and Type Four Errors. That is, we have solved the problem of preferring wishes to facts.) As Frank Rich wrote in the *New York Times*, "It's the power of the story that always counts first, and the selling of it that comes second. Accuracy is optional."[7] Wasn't Frey just giving his readers exactly what they wanted?

Sadly, our preference for unreality is indicated not only by the books, movie tickets, and other products and services we choose to purchase. We even "buy" candidates in a political process that has become almost devoid of content and substance. Our elections have become a gigantic game show, an endless series of cheap spectacles and one-liners from B-movies—but then so has every other aspect of modern life.

FIVE CRITICAL FACTORS

Five critical factors are primarily responsible for the rise of unreality and for our failure as a society to deal with it. They are also among some of the most potent factors responsible for the production and commission of Type Four Errors.

1. The Complexity of Modern Reality

Modern reality is far too complex for most of us to make sense of it. It is both figuratively and literally a mess. Recall once again that a mess is a "system of complex problems, all of which interact with and are part of one another."[8] We cannot emphasize too much that none of the problems that constitute the mess are independent of all the other problems.

For instance, the aftermath of Hurricane Katrina is not a single crisis or a single problem but rather a whole system of interrelated crises and problems that are connected in complex and baffling ways. Katrina is simultaneously a political, medical, evacuation, and housing problem—and more. Furthermore, none of these problems can be properly framed, let alone solved, independent of all the other problems. We invariably commit Type Three and Type Four Errors if we focus on one part or problem of a complex mess to the exclusion of all the other problems that constitute the mess. At our best, humans are mess managers. At our worst, we are mess mongers.

2. The Failure of Education and the Dumbing Down of America

We noted in Chapter Two that the educational system not only fails to teach us how to handle complex problems but actually miseducates us by spoon-feeding students a steady diet of simple exercises that have only one right answer. The result is not only the dumbing down of America but a country less and less able to think through complex problems, let alone handle megacrises.[9]

For example, at least in the beginning of the Iraq war, we uncritically accepted simpleminded assertions such as the oft-repeated claim by the Bush administration that "democracy reduces terrorism" when the relationship between the two is not only more complex and problematic than that but often in the opposite direction. The sad fact is that "more democracy" often furthers the rise of terrorism by providing extreme groups with legitimate access to the public marketplace of ideas. This is another example of more leading to less, which we discussed at length in Chapter Four.

In all our years of working with graduate students and senior executives, we have witnessed very few who are able to track on their own, without considerable help and encouragement, the complex relationships among even a small, limited number of factors. They are unable to foresee how even a few factors can interact to produce a major crisis. People are just not taught to think in terms of systems and complexity, but then they are rewarded for it even less.

3. A Stunning Array of Devices for Tuning Out Reality

The market has obligingly stepped into the gap between our inability to handle complexity and the overwhelming demands of reality with a dazzling and bewildering array of mindless reality TV shows, computer games, shopping malls, makeovers, and so on, all of which are designed to further entertain us, shield us, and anesthetize us from reality.

4. U.S. History and Culture

U.S. history and culture have also played prominent roles in turning Americans into the world's largest producers, consumers, and exporters of unreality. The United States was founded on myths that fuelled the rise of unreality. Two of the most fundamental myths were the beliefs that we were exempt from the laws of history and that we had a moral mandate to remake the world. Extreme makeovers are part of our heritage.[10]

5. The Failure to Think and Act Systemically

Just as we have a hard time thinking of the big picture, we also have a hard time acting on it. For example, every day we hear about new scientific breakthroughs regarding our ability to remake the human body. We can or we will soon be able to grow new biological replacements for hearts, lungs, even blood. We are also well down the road of being able to make artificial, that is, mechanical, replacements that are as good as or even better than the real thing. Not one scientist whom we have interviewed for this and other studies we have conducted has considered the effects of multiple augmentations and replacements on the human body as a total interconnected system. The heart specialists are doing their work independent of the lung specialists, who are working independent of the blood specialists, and so on. But the human body is one big, interconnected system; the heart neither exists nor functions independent of all the other organs. To ignore this fact is once again to deny complexity, and reality itself. It is, as we have emphasized repeatedly, not to solve the full problem. It constitutes Type Three and Type Four Errors of the first magnitude because it leaves us susceptible to unexamined issues within a complex set of problems.

SOME RECENT ILLUSTRATIONS

Although they already seem so distant as to be ancient history, the 2004 Republican and Democratic conventions are perfect examples of French social philosopher Jean Baudrillard's thesis that America is consumed by game shows and other trivia purporting to be reality.[11] Both conventions were a bizarre combination of two of the most popular TV "reality" shows: *Fear Factor* and *Extreme Makeover*. They were a case study in the masterful manipulation—by deliberate exaggeration—of genuine fears (of terrorism in the wake of 9/11) for partisan political gain. As if the Republican convention wasn't enough, within days vice president Dick Cheney warned us that if we didn't reelect the current administration, a new terrorist attack was almost certain. (As of 2009, Cheney is certain that it still is.) This was the TV game show *Fear Factor* played on the largest stage possible. The *Extreme Makeover* part of the election process was the disingenuous claim that the Republican Party and George W. Bush in particular were compassionate conservatives, that they really cared about minorities and the average working stiff, and that they and they alone could solve America's vast problems. On the Democratic side, it was the assertion that John Kerry and John Edwards would be even tougher and more effective on terrorism than Bush had been, and that they could rebuild (read "make over") the economy.

Both parties also played a combination of *Star Search*, by featuring the rising political stars of the moment, and *Hollywood Squares* ("my celebrities are bigger and better than yours") However, even this strategy wasn't enough to attract and hold the fickle attention of the masses, so they played *Survivor* as well. The winner, presumably, is no longer the person most qualified intellectually to be president but instead the person who is most popular, the person least likely to be voted off the island.

The same games were played out in the 2008 presidential election. Senator John McCain's selection of Sarah Palin as his running mate carried them to new lows.

MANUFACTURING UNREALITY

To understand how the Type Three and Type Four Errors are at the core of the media, and thus of today's world, let's take a deeper look at the mechanisms responsible for the creation and rise of unreality.

It is a strange but disconcerting fact that those who analyze the currently known and popular forms of unreality do not identify the general mechanisms that cut across and are found in virtually all forms of unreality. Without first seeing and analyzing these general mechanisms, we have no hope whatsoever of breaking unreality's grip. At best, most analyses treat only one or two types of unreality, such as video games, computer-generated forms of virtual reality, TV shows such as *Judge Judy* and *Survivor*, hyperreality chat rooms, and so on.[12] They also mainly treat them independent of the other forms. As a result, they fail to see and analyze unreality as a general phenomenon.

Like last season's game shows, particular types of unreality come and go, but the underlying mechanisms are enduring. These mechanisms are the "new realities" that underlie unreality.

THE PRINCIPAL MECHANISMS OF UNREALITY

To the best of our knowledge, seven major mechanisms are found in every form of unreality. Although not every one of these mechanisms is necessarily involved to the same degree, all of them are present in every form we have analyzed. Furthermore, although we have already touched on many of them, we need to take a deeper look at all of them. By doing this, not only will we get a better handle on the

nature of unreality, but we'll also in effect get an even better definition of it. The seven mechanisms are as follows:

1. Dumbing down: The pervasiveness of anti-intellectualism in
   American life

2. The radical reversal of the normal order: Unreality is more "real"
   and better than reality

3. The commercialization—that is, the selling—of everything

4. The immortality project: The radical rejection of reality, because
   reality is death

5. The radical conversion and transformation of all of reality into
   unreality

6. The acceptance and normalization of the bizarre and the
   antisocial

7. The misrepresentation and radical distortion of reality and truth:
   The blurring of boundaries

All of these major mechanisms are involved in every type of unreality because there are tremendous overlaps between them. They
are distinct only in the sense that they can be clearly identified and
named, not because they are independent. The list does not reflect
their order of importance, because there is none.

Also, because of the overlaps, it is not possible to discuss any of
the mechanisms separately. Each of the examples we give could be
used to discuss any and all of the mechanisms.

*The Radical Conversion and Transformation of
All of Reality into Unreality*
One of the most common, and seemingly most benign, forms of
unreality is *immersion*. (It is one end of a continuum; at the other
end is *conversion*.) In this form of unreality we become so immersed
in a computer game, an online chat room, YouTube, Second Life,
even a novel, and so on that it becomes more important than our
everyday lives. As a result, it takes precedence over reality. In the
extreme, it becomes reality.

All of us have had the experience of the characters in a game or novel becoming so real to us, of identifying with them so completely, that we feel we are literally part of them and they are part of us. We not only identify with them but take on their persona. In many cases, a person so identifies with a particular character that when the character dies the person feels that he or she has died as well. At the very least, a part of him or her has disappeared.

A simple example is the world of soap operas (although the "virtual world" of Second Life may be an even better example). Many people identify so strongly with the characters in a soap opera that they refuse to believe they are merely actors playing roles. Many viewers become so immersed in the lives of these characters that they believe they are real.

The by-now-ancient (1982) movie *Tron* is a perfect illustration of the mechanisms of immersion and conversion, of how they coexist and work together. In the movie, the main character, Kevin, becomes so involved—immersed—in playing a computer game that one day he is literally sucked into the computer. (This is the movie's main plot.) There he is converted into one of the players in the computer game. He is no longer a "real person." He has no existence outside of the computer.

Until he was sucked into the computer, Kevin could enter and exit the game at will simply by turning the computer on and off. Using the analogy of a swimming pool, he could dip into the water, so to speak, whenever he wanted to and emerge the same person he was before he entered the water. Being immersed in water did not fundamentally change his being human. However, as soon as he was sucked into the computer, he was no longer human. He could no longer emerge from the game simply by turning the computer off. The only way he could get out was by playing the game as one of the electronic characters and winning against all of the other characters. If he lost, he would be "terminated."

Another bizarre illustration of immersion is the well-documented case of "cyber-rape." One player-character was attacked and "raped" by another player-character. Even though all of this took place on a computer and no "real" people were involved or hurt physically, both players acted as if an actual physical attack had occurred. (The rape was committed through typed text, not in actual deed.) The larger community of players was so outraged by the incident that they expelled the offending member.[13] (Other recent examples unfortunately have involved "real" cases of teenagers being "cyber-bullied" unrelentingly by their peers and ending up committing suicide.)

The ultimate goal of this particular mechanism is not just to suck us deeper and deeper into unreality (deep immersion) but, stronger still, to convert or transform us into unreality. For example, an implicit and therefore not clearly recognized or understood goal of modern medicine is not merely to place computer chips in us to monitor our health and improve it, but to have us become one with and indistinguishable from the computer. In effect, we are to become the computer and the computer is to become us. As we mentioned earlier, the idea of the total replacement or enhancement of every part of the human body, of complete conversion, is no longer the stuff of science fiction. Not a day goes by that we don't learn of the invention of a new artificial device or body part. There are artificial bones, blood, hearts, hips, knees, kidneys, lungs, and so on. There seem to be no limits as to what we can do, want to do, and are willing to do to redesign and remanufacture humans to our specifications. This means that the day is fast approaching when, as we noted, we will in effect be able to become cyborgs. The questions are, *How will we tell that we have become cyborgs? Are there clear lines and crossover points dividing humans from machines?* And most disturbing of all, *Will we care?*

Apparently, a growing number of us *can't wait to mutate:*

FAKE IS BETTER: China chose its first Miss Artificial Beauty . . . giving the crown to a 22-year-old . . . who couldn't have done it without the help of her plastic surgeon.

Twenty contestants aged 17 to 62 competed in the final round of the "man-made beauty" pageant at a Beijing opera house, all having gone under the knife to improve their appearance.[14]

THE RADICAL REVERSAL OF THE NORMAL ORDER:
UNREALITY IS MORE "REAL" AND BETTER
THAN REALITY

The Immortality Project: The Radical Rejection
of Reality, Because Reality Is Death

If the body is nothing more than a sophisticated carrying case for the brain, and if the brain is in essence the true seat of the person, then why should a person die with the deterioration or death of the body? Why not upload the brain into a computer and then download it into a new and better body? And if we can do this, why not dispense with bodies altogether and just store all of us inside one big interconnected computer? Presumably this would free us not only from the tyranny of the body but from all international and social conflicts as well. According to this philosophy, the way to perfect humans lies in our continued perfection of technology. We say more about this in later chapters.

Time and time again, those who write about artificial, virtual, and cyber reality contend not only that unreality is better than reality but also that unreality *is* the new and superior reality. After all, isn't unreality better than death, the ultimate "bad reality"? In this way of thinking, death and complexity are viewed as opposite sides of the cosmic coin. The message is that unless we transform ourselves radically, we will have no control over either side.

The position can be stated even more strongly: It is our destiny to transform ourselves. We have a moral mandate to do so. For example, a recent article in *Wired* noted that

linking people via chip implants directly . . . machines seems a natural progression, a potential way of harnessing machine intelligence by, essentially, creating super humans.

I believe humans will become cyborgs and no longer be stand-alone entities. . . . [15]

In short, not only *ought* we to mutate because it's good for the future of the human race, but we *will* mutate because it's our destiny.

To put it mildly, unreality of this type is a radical social and political program. It represents a radical inversion of the moral order. Humans are almost totally devalued because machines (computers, cyborgs, and so on) are more important than and superior to people.

All of this can be summed up in a strange, if not bizarre, chain of reasoning:

In the beginning, the real is *the original, the authentic*, say, a Louis XIV chair; but then a copy, a fake, is made. The copy is so good that it looks even better than the original. It contains fewer defects. Its dimensions and shape are better, truer, and so on. Over time the artificial version comes to replace the original. At first, however, it is decried and put down as inferior. For, after all, it is a fake; it is not really real. But then, as more and more copies flood the market and become commonplace, they are regarded not only as better but as more real than the original.

This process is infinitely repeatable, and it extends into nature. Artificial environments such as shopping malls are considered better than nature itself. Not only can we control the weather inside, but we can also visit a scaled-down model of London and Paris any time we wish, without any hassles, cultural friction, or messy confrontations between those with whom we disagree ideologically and politically.

DUMBING DOWN: THE PERVASIVENESS OF ANTI-INTELLECTUALISM IN AMERICAN LIFE

The preceding point follows, of course, if and only if one accepts an incredible number of half-baked truths, faulty premises, dubious assumptions, and dumb arguments. Indeed, dumb arguments, most of which are unstated and therefore unexamined, are at the heart of unreality. In fact, the role of dumb arguments is the least examined aspect of unreality.

The put-down of intelligence and the celebration and elevation of lowbrow culture—except, of course, when brains can be used to make lots of money, as in *Who Wants to Be a Millionaire?*—are potent and never-ending sources of unreality. But anti-intellectualism has deep roots in U.S. history. This makes the United States especially fertile ground for unreality.

The following comment is a prime example of what we mean by a dumb argument. It was said in response to the pictures from Abu Ghraib. Its "unreality" boggles the mind: "Don't cheerleaders all over America form pyramids six to eight times a year? Is that torture?"[16]

The Commercialization—That Is, the Selling—of Everything
In the land of unreality, everything has its price and is therefore for sale, including the human body, news, privacy, public space, and childhood itself.

Recently, a man on eBay auctioned off his forehead as advertising space.

A Web designer who auctioned off the use of his forehead for advertising space is letting it go to his head.

Andrew Fischer, 20, of Omaha, who put his forehead on sale on eBay as advertising space, received $37,375 on Friday to advertise the snoring remedy SnoreStop.

"I look forward to an enjoyable association with Andrew—a man who clearly has a head for business in every sense of the word," SnoreStop's CEO Christian de Rivel said.

"People will always comment on something out of the ordinary," Fischer said in his sales pitch. "People like weird."[17]

Can the time be far off when ads will be implanted directly into people in the form of computer chips so they can beam their messages directly (in)to others? Or in the form of flashing message boards plastered onto their heads? Why not make the whole body into one gigantic walking ad? Why not give people free implants and replacement parts if they agree to advertise a particular manufacturer? Precisely because these proposals are so outrageous they are virtually guaranteed to happen.

The Acceptance and Normalization of
the Bizarre and the Antisocial
Increasingly, in all forms of unreality, the antisocial, the bizarre, and the pornographic are rendered normal and therefore acceptable. For

instance, the underlying message of the British unreality TV show *Big Brother* is that it is perfectly acceptable to be under constant surveillance. The notion of the surveillance society is legitimated by our willingness to submit to it freely.

Recently students at Harvard talked about starting a pornographic magazine and Web site in which they would be featured performers and spectators. A program on PBS's *Frontline* made the point repeatedly that the current generation of teenagers has few if any inhibitions. Revealing pictures of young girls that just a few generations ago would have been utterly unthinkable are now posted willingly on Facebook.

If anything could possibly be worse, surely it is the TV program 24, which normalizes torture. Indeed, torture has become exciting entertainment. Could exposure to programs like this help to explain, if only in part, and without in any way excusing the heinous acts committed, why the guards at Abu Ghraib were so easily drawn into torture, and especially why they didn't see it as such? The fact that adults and young people are more willing than ever to expose themselves on the Web (they do it every day) certainly helps to explain why the guards at Abu Ghraib had few inhibitions about posing with their captors in highly compromising positions. This is not meant to blame young people for Abu Ghraib. Instead, it is an attempt to understand how the media, widely construed, "influence" us. The word *influence* is key; we did not say "cause." The fact that reality is too complex to explain in terms of simple chains of cause and effect does not mean that there are not influences and, furthermore, that some "influences" are not more powerful than others.

Deception is a key feature of virtually all forms of unreality. In deception, what appears to be unscripted is actually scripted (here again we see the reversal of ordinary forms), such as when the producer of a television show carefully preselects certain types and mixes of participants, puts them in carefully controlled situations, feeds them lines, and films hours of tape that is then edited scrupulously to obtain a desired effect that is finally labeled "reality." In spite of knowing all of this—or because of it—people willingly accept fiction as fact. Which is fact and which is fiction no longer matters if it is entertaining and allows us, if only for a few moments, to escape the ultimate reality of death and boredom.

The Misrepresentation and Radical Distortion of Reality
and Truth: The Blurring of Boundaries
As we mentioned earlier, one of the most prominent features of all forms of unreality is the radical blurring of boundaries. For example, in computer games and chat rooms, on MTV, Facebook, and Second Life, and so on, one is "free" to assume multiple personalities and "try on" different genders and roles. In MTV in particular, dream states and ordinary waking states are mixed and blended so that they are virtually indistinguishable from one another. Indeed, such blurring is a prominent feature of MTV and computer games, and so forth. People are not only free to change sexes at will, but to be androgynous.

The boundaries between people and objects in such games are extremely fluid as well. Time, distance, and space are not fixed in any way but instead are broken down totally so that one is everywhere and nowhere at the same time.

The inside of shopping malls is so carefully controlled and staged that it looks and feels like outside (such as Paris or London), and such outside places as theme parks, for example, look and feel like inside. As a result, the concepts *outside* and *inside* don't mean anything any more.

The world of TV in particular misrepresents reality so that it becomes the "new reality." In TV dramas, people almost never die of natural causes. Blacks and other minorities are overrepresented as perpetrators of crime and live in poverty far beyond their actual numbers.

Unreality distorts death by oversanitizing and trivializing it, whether it occurs in actual wars or is simulated in video games, by suppressing its pain and gore. At the same time, unreality also amplifies death, as in video games that feature severed heads and limbs, sometimes with no blood or other consequences, other times with gallons of blood gushing forth. Unreality thus both intensi-fies and diminishes reality at the same time. The tension between the opposite poles of the human experience is one of the primary features of unreality. Of course this tension is also a major feature of reality.

A prime example of the intensification and misrepresentation of reality is how TV news in particular and the media in general de-monize the enemy or the opposition. Iraqi insurgents and soldiers are portrayed as not human like us. Neither are the criminals on cop shows. They therefore deserve to be mistreated. Everything is personalized and anthropomorphized. For example, U.S. war ma-chines are described in human terms and personified with names such as "the Retaliator."

On TV, all problems are portrayed as belonging to individuals. *Judge Judy* is a prime example. It shows welfare mothers as "bad" because they are personally irresponsible. (Shades of conservatism!) Society is never at fault. Institutional and societal racism doesn't exist. Racism exists only between individuals. Society as a complex system doesn't figure in at all. We are back to one of the classic dif-ferences between conservatives and liberals.[18]

Finally, all forms of unreality invent special terms and language in an attempt to confer legitimacy on themselves. For instance, the makers of *Judge Judy* view it as a "public service" program that aims to educate the public on the workings of the legal system. *Gamedocs* (a blend of documentaries and games in which a documentary is a game and vice versa), *chapelteria* (a cross between a chapel and a cafeteria), a *docudrama* (a dramatized documentary), *infotainment* (the blurring of information and entertainment), *edutainment* (the blurring of education and entertainment), and *dramality* (also dra-matized documentaries) are just a few of the oddball names and crossover terms that have been invented. Our personal favorite is *Biblezine*, which is a combination of a bible and a fashion magazine. Another favorite is *agritainment*. As farming has become more and more precarious as a form of making a living, farmers have increas-ingly turned their farms into entertainment theme parks.

ONE CAN NEVER BE TOO OUTRAGEOUS

Not only was satirist Terry Southern far ahead of his time in antici-
pating unreality, but he also had a surefire method for predicting the
forms it would assume. The method is *outrageousness:*

Before dinner [Guy] Grand completed arrangements begun earlier in the
day with the Chicago stockyards: the delivery of three hundred cubic feet
of manure, a hundred gallons of urine, and fifty gallons of blood to [an
isolated location in the suburbs where it was then transported by truck
and finally dumped into a large vat in downtown Chicago]. . . .

. . . [Grand] squatted on the [edge] of the vat [of the stinking mess]
and opened [a] briefcase, out of which he began taking, a handful at a
time, and dropping into the vat, ten thousand one-hundred-dollar bills,
slowly stirring them in with his wooden paddle.

. . . Then he stepped down, opened [a] can of paint, gave it a good
stirring, and finally, using his left hand so that what resulted looked child-
ish or illiterate, he scrawled across the vat FREE $ HERE in big black let-
ters on the sides facing the street.

The commotion that occurred a few hours later . . . was the first and,
in a sense, the most deliberately literal of such projects eventually to be
linked with the name of "Grand Guy" Guy Grand, provoking the wrath
of the public press against him. . . . [19]

When it comes to predicting the future, artists are generally far
ahead of everyone else. Unlike most of us, they are not fettered by
facts or convention. They are better able to see the awful future
that lies ahead for humankind because they place no constraints
on their imagination.

As the preceding fragment from Southern's *The Magic Christian*
demonstrates, nearly a half-century ago he anticipated that people
would do the most vile things for money. He foresaw clearly that
people would happily "bob" for money in vats of excrement. With
an uncanny, if not spooky, sense of the future, he also anticipated
most of today's other game show formats. For instance, in a show
he called *What's My Disease?* a contestant appears on stage in front
of a panel of doctors. If one of the doctors can correctly guess the

contestant's disease or problem, the contestant gets a free operation on the spot in front of a live audience. Similarities with the following are intentional:

The Fox network, which drew complaints earlier this year for reality shows about gay imposters and a dwarf looking for his bride, has provoked an organized campaign against its newest reality-show creation, *Who's Your Daddy?*

In the show, an adult woman adopted as an infant has a chance to win $100,000 if she can correctly choose her biological father from among eight men, including seven imposters. If she chooses a fake, he will win the money. . . . [20]

Southern anticipated the likes of Jerry Springer. In one particularly hilarious and cruel scene, Guy Grand flies above a large crowd shouting obscene racial and ethnic epithets at them. He provokes the people to turn viciously on one another. This has of course been his intent all along.

In another scene, Grand engages the current heavyweight boxing champion of the world and the top challenger to stage a fight. Instead of sparring normally, both fighters prance about the ring as if they were stereotypically gay, throwing mock blows at one another and recoiling hysterically from exaggerated swishes that obviously miss their target. At first the crowd is dumfounded. They don't know what to make of this behavior and how to react. Finally they explode in uncontrollable anger and disgust. Mayhem ensues. Once again Grand has prevailed by exploiting the base instincts and crude prejudices of the "public," read "mob."

Southern's basic device for identifying the absurdities (or unrealities) that underlie the human condition is to use extreme ridicule by being completely outrageous. (Today we would say by being extremely "politically incorrect.") Thus, the strategy is that anyone who wishes to predict the future is advised to be as outrageous and polemical as possible. In fact, one cannot be too outrageous. To the contrary, as soon as one thinks one has been too outrageous or outrageous enough, one has failed. Ratchet it up five more notches.

By ridiculing virtually all of our sacred beliefs, prejudices, and foibles—by taking them to absurd levels—Southern essentially anticipated all of the game shows that would later be known as reality shows. In other words, without being aware of our terms, he anticipated the major forms of Type Three and Type Four Errors committed by the media. Nonetheless, as prescient as he was, Southern did not anticipate, and therefore did not identify, the common mechanisms that all of the various types of unreality share.

CONCLUDING REMARKS

In an ideal if not overly simplified and simplistic world, problems would consist of clearly defined means and ends, or more generally, causes and effects. Furthermore, the means and ends would be distinct and distinguishable from one another. The trouble is, we don't now live in such a world, if we ever did.

The world in which we live is one in which means and ends (causes and effects) are inextricably intertwined. The means not only produce the ends, but the ends themselves are their very own means, and the means are their own ends. It is a world in which problems, means, and ends are mixed and intermixed in complex, perplexing, and difficult-to-understand ways. For example, consider the particular mechanism of dumbing down. Dumbing down is not only a *means* for producing unreality, but it is also one of the prime characteristic features of unreality. It is therefore an *end* or *outcome* of unreality as well. It is a means because it renders us increasingly unable to handle complex ideas, and therefore reality itself. It is an end because dumbing down leads only to more of itself. Finally, dumbing down is a Type Four Error because it is the solution to the problem of how to dumb down a whole society.

6

THE WONDERFUL WORLD
OF ACADEMIA
Misrepresenting Reality

Nature is not organized in the same way that universities are.

—RUSSELL ACKOFF

A DIFFERENT KIND OF EDUCATION

In June 1967, Mitroff obtained his doctorate in engineering science
from the University of California at Berkeley, with a special minor
in the philosophy of social systems science. He was the first, and to
our knowledge the only, student ever to take such a minor in the
College of Engineering. Instead of being encouraged to branch out
and round out his education, he was in fact challenged constantly
by the administration of the College to justify what social science,
let alone philosophy, had to do with engineering. The short answer
is, *Everything!*

Sadly, forty years later, Mitroff has returned to Berkeley, where
he is now part of an interdisciplinary research group that studies
large-scale disasters such as Katrina, and nothing much has changed.
Despite all the talk about the necessity for interdisciplinary research, teaching, and collaboration, the overwhelming majority of
engineers and academics are still reluctant to venture much beyond

their chosen disciplines and subspecialties. This is the case in spite of the research that demonstrates that the vast majority of engineering failures are due to human and organizational errors, not to the breakdown and failure of technology alone.

In this chapter we concentrate on two aspects of higher education that in our judgment contribute most to Type Three and Type Four Errors. The first aspect is the deeply held belief that physical and social phenomena *can be* strictly separated from one another. In the extreme version of this belief, physical and social phenomena not only *are* but *must be* totally separated—that is, they exist in completely different realms and therefore can't help but be independent of each other.

The second aspect is the belief, also deeply held, that knowledge can be partitioned into "hard" and "soft" sciences, and furthermore, that the "hard sciences" are superior to the "soft sciences." To demonstrate the erroneousness of these beliefs, we tell briefly the story of Mitroff's research for his doctorate in engineering.

SIMULATING A SINGLE ENGINEER

Mitroff's doctoral dissertation involved building a computer model that would *simulate* (the technical term for "match") as closely as possible the design behavior of a single engineer.[1] The goal was to reproduce as much as possible the designs that an actual engineer—we call him "Bill"—produced.

Bill's job was to design a pressure vessel—a metal container—that would fit snugly around a plastic flask containing liquid hydrogen. Because hydrogen is highly explosive if it interacts with oxygen, one of the pressure vessel's main purposes was to keep air from getting into the flask and mixing with the hydrogen. Not only did the pressure vessel have to keep air out of the flask, but it also had to be strong enough to contain and minimize the damage from an explosion.

The best way to think of a pressure vessel is to imagine the walls of a balloon. Although they are extremely thin and malleable (stretchable), they are strong enough to contain the increase in internal air pressure that results when we blow up the balloon. They do so by developing a counterbalancing force—or more accurately, stress.[2] We see this literally in the balloon's expansion.

The same thing happens in a metal pressure vessel if the pressure inside it is increased. However, because its walls are much thicker and stronger than the walls of a balloon, the metal vessel does not stretch as much, at least not to a degree perceptible to the naked eye. Nonetheless, if one uses precise instruments to measure the vessel's dimensions, one finds that if the pressure inside the vessel is increased, then the metal has indeed stretched, albeit by a very small amount. Thus, the walls of a pressure vessel, like the walls of a balloon, develop a counterbalancing stress to contain the internal pressure. If the internal pressure becomes too great, the vessel expands until, like a balloon, it cannot do so anymore and, finally, explodes.

The pressure vessel that Bill was to design had to perform another critical function as well. Because extremely low temperatures are required to keep hydrogen in a liquid state, the air inside the vessel had to be pumped out to create an internal vacuum. When this happened, the outside air pressure could crush the vessel. Therefore, its walls had to be thick enough to withstand both an internal explosion and the external force produced by the outside atmospheric pressure. (This is precisely why it is called a pressure vessel.)

Thus Bill's job was simultaneously to make the walls of the vessel as thin as possible, to allow for expansion, and as thick as possible, to resist the external atmospheric pressure and the internal pressure of an explosion, and thereby satisfy the needs of his clients.

Bill's clients were highly sophisticated. In fact, they had doctorates in nuclear physics. They were studying the nuclear properties of liquid hydrogen. To accomplish this, they shot intense beams of nuclear particles at high energies into the hydrogen flask. The atomic properties of hydrogen were to be determined by the particles that resulted from the collisions between the incoming particles and the hydrogen in the flask.

The difficulty of Bill's task was as follows: if he made the walls of the pressure vessel too thick but safe, the physicists would end up studying the nuclear properties of the vessel instead of the hydrogen. On the other hand, if he made the walls too thin, he risked crushing the vessel and causing an explosion. There was no best solution to this situation. Every design that Bill came up with was a compromise.

In addition to balancing these two conflicting demands, Bill was juggling other, equally important considerations. If he made the walls of the vessel out of an exotic material such as beryllium, he could make them thinner than if he made them out of stainless steel, and thus allow the physicists to perform their job even better, that is, get stronger experimental results more quickly. However, making the vessel out of beryllium would increase dramatically the cost of manufacturing the vessel. Because most people, including physicists, have to work within the constraints of a budget, they were limited in how much money they could spend in unlocking Mother Nature's secrets.

The Real Story

The real story, however, is only beginning. It took more than a year of Bill and Mitroff working closely together as a research team to flesh out as many of Bill's design rules as they could. The task was difficult because many of the rules were implicit, so Bill was not fully conscious of all of them. They worked so closely together that they had to abandon the traditional distinction between Mitroff as the supposedly "objective researcher" and Bill as the supposedly "subjective subject." They became co-researchers so they could study Bill as their "collective subject." In fact, this was the only way they could justify Bill's devoting so much time to the project. Bill had to stand to gain something real and very important from the project— a deeper understanding of his own design behavior. To help ensure that this would happen, Mitroff required Bill's full cooperation. There was no way he could get at Bill's rules by observing Bill from afar. Mitroff also learned, however, that he had to give up the illusion of complete objectivity, the pretense that he was a totally objective researcher.

Testing Bill and the Computer Program

After about a year of working together, Mitroff had put enough of Bill's design rules into a computer that they were ready to test Bill's behavior against the computer. The day finally came when the computer and Bill were fed the same series of typical design situations.

Working separately, the computer and Bill responded. Bill and Mitroff then compared the computer's responses with Bill's. What transpired next was absolutely astounding. Neither Bill nor Mitroff had anticipated it in the slightest. Because the computer was able to perform many more complex calculations in a much shorter time than a human could ever possibly accomplish, it was able to generate many more design alternatives than Bill could that could potentially satisfy the physicists' needs. When Bill looked at the computer's responses, he saw immediately that the computer was producing many more designs than he had ever considered, and many of them were better than his. As a result, Bill decided on the spot to use the computer on a regular basis as a new and improved design tool.

But here's the rub: *the computer model was initially developed to "simulate"* Bill, *but a number of the designs that the computer produced were so superior that* Bill *ended up simulating the computer. In effect, the roles had become completely reversed. It was no longer clear who was simulating whom.* Bill *decided to use the computer as a design tool precisely because it was performing not only differently from but also superior to his original behavior.*

Mitroff had unwittingly and unknowingly discovered the distinction between artificial intelligence (AI) and artificial life (AL) some twenty years before the field of AL was invented. In AI, the human is the standard, or *fundamental reality*, that we aspire to simulate. In AL, the machine is now the standard, or fundamental reality, which humans aspire to emulate. Bill's decision to adopt the computer model as a design aid was in effect a decision to yield to a new and improved reality.

However, in the spirit of the preceding chapter, what indeed is "real"? To capture the full "reality" of the situation, do we also need to simulate the simulator, that is, Mitroff? Does Mitroff's behavior as a researcher also need to be simulated by someone else? In capturing Bill's design rules, Mitroff was following certain implicit rules of his own. One way to test how good a job Mitroff was doing would be to compare his behavior with a computer simulation of him, and on and on, ad nauseam.

LESSONS

In the years since Mitroff built the computer simulation of Bill's behavior, the authors have ruminated on the many lessons that were learned. The first and most important lesson was that engineering is as much an art as it is a science—but what isn't? Still, to those outside the profession, engineering appears to be an exact science, that is, an activity governed through and through by impersonal objective formulas. Engineers are viewed as the epitome of rational beings. In fact, the profession often deliberately promotes this image to its political and social advantage. The truth, however, is far different.

The fact that engineering is an art was constantly brought home to Mitroff in two ways. The first way was primarily technical; the second was primarily social and ultimately systemic.

On the surface, Bill's job was inordinately simple. Because the vast majority of hydrogen flasks were spheres or cylinders, the surrounding pressure vessels could be either spheres or cylinders as well. If anything is simple from an engineering standpoint, it is the design of spherical and cylindrical vessels. The formulas for calculating the necessary thickness of the walls in spherical and cylindrical pressure vessels are among the simplest in all of science and engineering. (That these formulas are so simple is precisely what seduces so many people into believing that engineering and science are founded on the twin pillars of objective data and observations and hard-nosed rationality. Because such people ignore the human and social contexts in which engineering and science exist, they are blind to their systems aspects.)

From a purely technical standpoint, then, Bill's job should have been easy. The task of building a computer program of his behavior should have been completed in weeks, not months. But other influences were operating to make Bill's job more complicated.

One difficulty was that not all of the flasks were in fact simple spheres or cylinders. Thus the formulas for calculating the necessary thicknesses of the walls were complicated. Yet this wasn't the real source of the difficulties.

NOT ALL PHDS ARE EQUAL

The real sources of Bill's difficulty were social factors. Although all of Bill's clients had their doctorates in physics, not all doctorates are equal. It makes a tremendous difference whether one has a relatively new degree or is an older, more mature physicist. In general, the older, more experienced, and more prestigious a physicist is, the better will be the engineering designs he or she receives from an engineer such as Bill.

On the whole, the younger physicists among Bill's clients were insecure. As a result, they generally approached Bill with their own designs. Because they knew much more about physics than Bill did, they assumed they also knew much more about engineering. How wrong they were. Therein lay their downfall. Their faulty assumptions led them to solve the wrong problem. By imposing their designs on Bill, the younger physicists were in effect committing Type Three Errors by not letting Bill define the problem. That is, they were fooling themselves.

Bill looked at the designs that the younger physicists wanted and replied sarcastically with a version of, "Yes, Sir, Master!" If he said it once he said it hundreds of times, "I *always* give my clients what they *ask for* even if it's not what they *need*!" Bill knew that by building exactly what an inexperienced physicist requested, and in many cases demanded, of him he would be ruining their experiments. Because they were treating him with disdain, Bill was deliberately getting back at them by playing a game of spite. In effect, Bill was taking the younger physicists' designs and forcing them back on them as Type Four Errors. Depending, of course, on one's point of view, one doesn't have to be a dirty rotten scoundrel to commit Type

Four Errors. The younger physicists' designs almost always ended up with much thicker walls than would have been the case if they had let Bill design them. They would have to run their experiments much longer to get the results they desired, if they ever could.

In comparison, the older, more experienced, more mature, and generally much more prestigious physicists—a number were Nobel Prize winners—assumed the exact opposite from the younger physicists. Although they obviously knew more about physics, they assumed that Bill knew much more about engineering than they did. They basically trusted him to come up with the designs they needed.

No wonder it took more than a year to get all of Bill's design rules into a computer; they were a highly complex mixture of engineering formulas tempered by the informal and implicit social rules of the game.

Because all of the designs had to be justified, they had to be accompanied by an engineering analysis of some kind. This was necessary even for the designs that were thrust upon him by the younger physicists. The joke in all of this was that Bill could almost pick whatever formula he wanted to justify whatever design he produced.[3] He could thus disguise the Type Four Errors he was making. (This was long before Mitroff was even aware of the Type Four Error.)

IDEAL MODELS

One of the reasons that lay people generally assume that engineering is an exact science is that they believe, erroneously, that every physical phenomenon is governed by a single, well-defined equation or formula. Nothing could be further from the truth. (Recall the discussion in Chapter Two about exercises.)

All of the formulas and equations in science and engineering are approximations. They are based on ideal models that greatly simplify a situation so that a mathematical theory of it can be constructed. The real world is generally so complicated that it is literally impossible to model it completely, but because different models often make radically different assumptions about the nature of the world, different formulas are possible.

In the real world (given the discussion in the last chapter, what is real is less certain than ever), one is never dealing with perfect spheres or perfect materials. Real pressure vessels do not always behave as ideal, theoretical ones do. For this reason, one has to test the ideal equations against the ones that result from laboratory tests. There is often a good agreement between experiment and theory. In fact, in most cases theory is modeled after the results of experiments. Many times, however, there is a significant gap between theory and experiment. When this happens, one gets a different formula based on analyses of the experimental results. Bill therefore chose, sometimes consciously but many times unconsciously, which formula a particular physicist got for the design of his or her pressure vessel. Again, depending on the formula that was chosen, a physicist could end up getting a pressure vessel with either thin walls or thick walls. If a physicist got a pressure vessel with walls thicker than were needed for his or her experiment, it could end up ruining the experiment. Even though practicing engineers and savvy engineering professors knew this happened all the time, from the standpoint of traditional engineering the situation Mitroff was studying was absolutely outrageous. That is, in principle the equations of science and engineering are not supposed to depend on any personal or social factors at all. The vaunted objectivity of engineering requires that physical formulas and results not depend on inherently subjective factors such as the age, sex, education, attitudes, and so on of a client or designer. Yet in reality this was exactly what was happening.

THE STRICT COMPARTMENTALIZATION
OF PHENOMENA

The academic and professional worlds generally believe in and adhere to the strict compartmentalization of phenomena. Thus social phenomena are the exclusive province of the social sciences and the humanities while physical phenomena are the exclusive province of the physical sciences and engineering.

The academic and professional worlds also generally believe that the various fields of knowledge can be arrayed from the "best" down to the "worst." Thus the physical sciences, logic, mathematics, and engineering are generally regarded as the most prestigious subjects taught and studied in universities. Presumably this is because they are the most rigorous and exact sciences. The social sciences generally enjoy much less prestige. Supposedly they are subject to changing social taste and fashion. They are also (erroneously) believed to be much less precise than the physical sciences. Yet Mitroff's study shows that this neat and comforting division of the world doesn't hold at all. In fact, this is one of the major findings of Mitroff's dissertation research. The two worlds are inextricably bound together.

Of course this result has been found again and again. Mitroff is certainly not the only one to have observed this state of affairs. The trouble is that this finding is still not as widely accepted as it should be in the design and operation of universities.

IMPLICATIONS

The findings of Mitroff's dissertation have profound implications for whether computers and other machines can simulate or replace humans. For instance, it is often assumed that we can simulate the behavior of an individual in isolation from all social influences. Yet Mitroff's study of Bill demonstrated unequivocally that Bill's behavior and rules could not be captured apart from the behavior and rules of his clients and of the larger social system of which they were parts.

The strongest conclusion is that *it is impossible to simulate a single mind independent of and in isolation from all other minds, that is, in isolation from the larger system, or mess, to which it is connected. To build a complete computer model of a single mind requires that we also build a complete computer model of all the other minds to which it is connected and on which it depends for its existence and sustenance.* The concept of *mind* is thus inherently systemic, social as well as cultural.

The mind is not solely physical, although no one would deny that it has physical aspects. Another way to put it is to say that although the brain is in the head, the mind is spread throughout a person's body as well as the body of society. The upshot is that any time we build models of complex phenomena that are anything less than systemic, we commit Type Three and Type Four Errors.

BUSINESS SCHOOL EDUCATION
AND THE APPLIED SOCIAL SCIENCES

One would think that because the social sciences purportedly deal with people and organizations, the erroneous belief that one can separate technology and people would be vastly different, if not superior, especially in the applied social sciences, such as business administration, which have to deal with exceedingly complex circumstances. One would think that by necessity they would incorporate a much more highly refined and sophisticated view of humans and organizations. Although this is indeed the case in many parts of the social sciences, such as clinical psychology and organizational change dynamics, it is not the case throughout.

Two of the most prominent theories of business—*transaction cost analysis* and *agency theory*—are taught and researched in virtually every school of business around the world. They are built on *a mean-spirited and distorted view of human nature* and on *a narrow, outdated, and repudiated notion of ethics*. Although business educators and researchers are not directly responsible for the scandals—such as Enron and, more recently, the credit crisis—that have racked the business world in recent years, they are contributing and enabling factors.

Although the reasons for this state of affairs are many and complex, a good part of the explanation has to do with the assumption that some fields of knowledge (such as economics) are not only better than others (such as ethics) but are completely separate from them.[4] According to this line of thinking, economics is better than ethics because economics is a hard-nosed and rigorous science whereas ethics is inherently soft and squishy.

Without going into the details of transaction cost analysis and agency theory, we can say that both of them assume that human beings are, at their core, entirely ruthless and motivated solely by greed. That is, both theories assume that people are completely opportunistic and selfish, that they are solely out for themselves and for no one else. This assumption is the basis for our charge that current business theories are built on a mean-spirited and distorted view of human nature. To assume otherwise—that is, that human beings are generous and altruistic—makes it much harder to construct theories of business. Thus, too many business educators and researchers have consciously or unconsciously chosen to solve a "simple" problem rather than an accurate or "true" one. At best, this choice represents a Type Three Error. It becomes a Type Four Error when business educators and researchers try to convince the rest of the world that their theories are powerful if not true and scientifically valid means for understanding and running businesses—and the economy in general.

Now, the assumption that people are opportunistic and selfish certainly applies to humans, but to assume that it applies 100 percent of the time is both preposterous and outrageous. If people *were* motivated solely by greed and completely opportunistic, selfish, and so on 100 percent of the time, it explains why current economic thought and theories of business find it extremely difficult to explain how altruism can arise. It's akin to starting with the assumption that everyone is a cold-blooded, ruthless murderer, and then trying to explain how anyone but a few individuals would be left alive.

If one starts with the assumption that human beings are mean and, further, that meanness begets meanness, then how could any of the other virtues that human beings possess possibly exist, let alone have arisen in the first place?

EGOISM

One of the earliest theories of ethics, founded more than two thousand years ago, is *egoism*, which assumes that the only thing that truly motivates people is self-interest. It should come as no surprise that contemporary moral philosophers have refuted egoism, because at best the concept of "self-interest" is unclear, and at worst it often leads to actions that are not in one's "self-interest." It's not that egoism and self-interest don't apply at all but, again, that they don't apply all of the time.

What does *self-interest* mean? As innumerable human actions— most notably addiction—show, we do not always act in ways that are in our own best interest. But if pure egoism were true, how could trust, without which society is not possible, develop and sustain itself? How could egoism possibly account for the following, for example, except of course by the tortuous argument that altruism is actually in one's self-interest?

People wondered, because they had asked themselves, "Could I have done what he did?" and very often the answer was "no." Mr. Autrey, 50, a construction worker and Navy veteran, leapt in front of a train to rescue a stranger who had suffered a seizure and fallen onto the tracks. He covered the stranger's body with his own as the train passed overhead. Both men lived.

. . . One of the curious aspects about Mr. Autrey's deed is that he jumped even though his daughters, ages 4 and 6, were at his side. Normally, experts say, the power of the parent-child dynamic would overwhelm any tendency to put yourself in harm's way to rescue a stranger. Then again . . . people who already feel attachment, like the kind toward their children, may be predisposed to act more altruistically to others. . . .

Considering that people tend to act more altruistically toward those who fall within their perceived group . . . it was notable that differences in race—Mr. Autrey is black, [the victim] is white—didn't enter the picture.

"Not only is he going beyond the narrow interest that we all seem to have toward our children, but he is reaching out toward a shared common humanity. And, he's doing it across a racial line," Dr. Post [professor of bioethics at Case Western Reserve University] said."[5]

We find it extremely sad that generally the only business books that treat such issues are the so-called touchy-feely, popular ones. True, many of these books are simple-minded and trite and thus do not deserve to be taken seriously, but the entire phenomenon of altruism does not warrant being dismissed out of hand by the academy, and neither do all of these books.

At best our current theories of business are founded on an outmoded ethical theory. At worst they assume that there has been no progress at all in the two thousand years since egoism was first proposed.

Many business school faculties make a number of unfounded assumptions and assertions about the field of ethics. First, they assert that ethics is nothing but a matter of one's underlying values. In other words, ethics is solely about values and nothing else. Second, they assume that by the time one gets to business school, one's values are fixed and rigid. Third, they assume that it is the role of one's parents and religious instructors, and not of business school faculty, to teach values. In other words, business faculties have little if any role in teaching values.

These assumptions are wrong. First, ethics is not primarily about values, although values certainly enter in. How could they not? Second, ethics is fundamentally about justifying one's values in light of the arguments and challenges that various theories of ethics address to them. In other words, ethics is primarily about clarifying and defending our values through reasoned argument and debate. Third, our values are not fixed. If they were, the possibility of human development over the course of our lives would be absolutely precluded. (See Chapter Eight.) Finally, it would be much easier to accept the assertion that business school faculties do not act in the role of surrogate priests or rabbis if they were not promulgating their own values—ruthlessness, selfishness, and so on—through the theories they have developed. Again, the base on which these theories are built is not only narrow but invalid.

ETHICAL ACCOUNTING AND FINANCE

The preceding points were made a few years ago by distinguished sociologist Amitai Etzioni. In an op-ed piece he wrote for the *Washington Post*, Etzioni recounted his experience as a visiting professor at the Harvard Business School, where he taught a one-year course in ethics. At the end of his time there, a meeting was held for the entire faculty to discuss whether the course in ethics should be continued. Some of the discussion was downright bizarre. A number of the finance faculty said openly, "If we teach a course in business ethics, it will only show that what I am teaching is unethical. Ergo, . . ."

We have no doubt as to the accuracy of Etzioni's observations. If a large body of faculty shares them, then we are truly in deep trouble.

Notice what the Harvard faculty members were doing. Instead of choosing the problem of how to create academic and professional fields of *ethical* accounting and finance, which is anything but an oxymoron, they instead chose the problem of how to create *un*ethical fields of accounting and finance. Talk about dirty rotten scoundrels! We rest our case as to the Type Four Errors committed in the name of objective academic research and debate.

A TELLING BLOW

An even more telling blow to economics are the following comments; unfortunately one of the key concepts of economics, the concept of *rational economic man*, applies more to apes than it does to humans:

Economic theory has contrived a species it calls *Homo economicus*—a "rational maximizer" who grabs what he can for himself.

[However, in experiments, p]eople do not act like *Homo economicus*. Instead, they are the arbiters of fairness.

. . . [In experiments] chimps are simply rational maximizers—*Pan economicus*, if you like.[6]

The conclusion? We have developed the kind of economics that applies mainly to apes. Why? Because it is founded, whether knowingly or unknowingly, on the behavior of apes. The time is far overdue to develop the kind of economics that applies to humans.

ANOTHER EXAMPLE

A few years ago, Mitroff chaired a doctoral qualifying exam for an extremely bright and gifted student. Needless to say, the student passed with flying colors. Nonetheless, one aspect of the exam was highly disturbing. It revealed another example of how the academic world perpetuates Type Four Errors.

Because the student was obviously intelligent and talented, many of the typical doctoral exam questions were bypassed entirely. Instead, a considerable part of the exam was devoted to the student's proposed dissertation topic.[7]

A number of the faculty noted that the topic cut across the fields of organization behavior, organization theory, and business strategy. Although they didn't wish to preclude the student outright from tackling such a broad subject, they raised serious concerns about the student's "welfare." They were concerned that pursuing this topic would make it difficult for the student to get an academic job. A number of the faculty members noted that they themselves had experienced considerable trouble when they pursued similar topics early in their doctoral careers. They stated that their comments were intended to "help" the student. That is, they didn't want to prohibit the student from undertaking the topic; they just wanted to warn the student about the possible dangers of doing so.

Although organization behavior, organization theory, and business strategy deserve to be taken seriously, they should not be reified. That is, we should not act as if they are totally separate components of human experience. They are not. They are merely convenient categories that we have created in order to distinguish different aspects of human behavior from one another. They help us to manage our world. They are not real or distinct in themselves.

We should be encouraging those students who are capable to undertake topics that bridge the categories we have created, not putting barriers in their way and discouraging them. To the extent that we do the latter, is it any wonder that we have produced so few minds that are capable of bridging diverse aspects of management, let alone of human affairs?

CONCLUDING REMARKS

Humans form deep bonds with their models and machines. They are highly dependent on them. However, some models are not worth bonding with. We bond with certain models at our peril.

The worst thing about transaction cost analysis and agency

theory is not that they are clearly false given that they make errone-ous assumptions about people. The worst thing is that by adopting them we make them true, and by doing so we commit an enormous Type Four Error. No better illustration can be given than the recent housing market meltdown. We have constructed a whole economy based on the most efficient solution to the wrong problem—how to maximize uncontrolled greed.

We can only expect the dependency among humans, their ma-chines, their theories, and their models to grow, not to diminish. This is especially true in a world that is increasingly interconnected along every conceivable dimension. It is so interconnected that, as we noted before, Thomas Friedman refers to it as "flat."[8] Yet the relationship among humans, machines, theories, and models is even stronger than that. This and the previous chapter have shown that *we are well on the way to becoming one with our models and ma-chines. In a word, we are becoming our models and machines, and they are becoming us.* Not only are we bonding with our machines, but we are also *fusing* with them. *They are essentially becoming part of our genetic makeup.*

POSTSCRIPT

This chapter vividly illustrates that no science or branch of knowledge is more fundamental than any other, and every science and branch of knowledge is dependent on every other.

Look at how in this chapter Bill's supposedly hard-nosed engi-neering formulas and design procedures depended heavily on messy and soft psychological and social factors. This is why the philoso-pher, E. A. Singer Jr.—like his mentor, distinguished Harvard phi-losopher William James—regarded the distinction between *soft* and *hard* and between *objective* and *subjective* as false, naive, misleading, and worst of all, dangerous. As we saw in Chapter Four, the opera-tion of complex and dangerous technologies are all too dependent on equally complex humans and social systems.

The division of the world into hard and soft sciences and branches of knowledge is itself a distinction that is "too soft" for today's world. By labeling some fields hard, and therefore more basic, we retard the advancement of knowledge, and reality, or certainly our ability to manage it, is thus retarded as well. This division is one of the biggest Type Four Errors we can commit. It leads us to believe that the problems of some disciplines are better, more important, or more fundamental than the problems of other disciplines.

British philosopher Mary Midgley has put it well:

We need scientific pluralism—the recognition that there are many independent forms and sources of knowledge—rather than reductivism, the conviction that one fundamental form underlies them all and settles everything.[9]

7

THE ABUSE AND MISUSE
OF SCIENCE

Baruch Fischhoff, professor of social and decision sciences at Carnegie Mellon University, recently asked a panel of 20 communications and finance experts what they thought the likelihood of human-to-human transmission of avian flu would be in the next three years. They put the figure at 60%. He then asked a panel of 20 medical experts the same question. Their answer: 10%. "There's reason to be critical of experts," Fischhoff says, "but not to replace their judgment with laypeople's opinions."[1]

A SUPERIOR FORM OF KNOWLEDGE
Science is regularly touted as a superior method and form of knowledge. Indeed, it is regularly claimed that it is superior to all other forms of knowledge.

Although science is certainly one of the best ways that humans have ever invented for producing knowledge, it is not the only way. Furthermore, as an institution and as a method and a form of knowledge, science is not free from flaws. Naturally this does not mean that science is on an equal footing with, say, creationism.

In this chapter we take a critical look at science's philosophical underpinnings in order to show that science contains significant elements that, according to its own strict standards, are "non-scientific." It is precisely by studying itself as critically as it studies everything else that science, to its immense credit, reveals the "irrational" and "subjective" elements that are embedded within it. It also finds that these very elements serve a positive and vital purpose. They are not only necessary but rational in a broad sense.

Studying the philosophical underpinnings of science yields other important benefits as well. For example, it reveals a way to assess when we are committing Type Three and Type Four Errors. This is in fact one of the most important outcomes presented in this chapter.

Just as important, this chapter is about much more than science alone. It is concerned primarily with how we think. In other words, although studying the philosophical underpinnings of science is important in its own right, it is also a convenient way to study how we think about problems in general. For this reason, we give examples not only from science but also from everyday life.

THE SUBJECTIVITY OF SCIENTISTS

In 1974, Mitroff published *The Subjective Side of Science,* an intensive behind-the-scenes study of the Apollo moon scientists over the course of the Apollo missions.[2] It showed in no uncertain terms how science really works. It demonstrated that science is not fully rational, and that scientists are not the perfectly objective and rational creatures they have been portrayed as. They are certainly not free from all biases. Indeed, one of the most important findings of this study was that science would grind to a complete halt if scientists were free from all biases. (A host of other studies have shown the same results repeatedly.[3])

For instance, does anyone seriously believe that the scientists who were bold, creative, and smart enough to develop theories on the origin of the moon would give up those pet theories just because the first rocks to be brought back from the moon did not support them? Not at all. They did everything in their power to reinterpret the evidence so that it would support their theories. They contended, and with justification, that we had not sampled the moon's entire surface and therefore had not yet proved beyond all doubt that their theories were false. They even reformulated their theories so that the evidence would fit with their original ideas.

Every single one of the top forty-two scientists whom Mitroff interviewed repeatedly over the course of the Apollo moon missions argued strongly that outright bias plays a crucial role in science. It would not serve science well if scientists abandoned their pet theories too soon. They should do so only after they have done everything in their power to preserve those theories and only after the evidence against them is finally overwhelming—a process that could take years.

Objectivity—one of the great hallmarks of science—is not a property of individual scientists. Indeed, completely unbiased scientists do not exist. In fact, in a study done some years ago, it was shown that Protestant ministers actually followed the dictates of the scientific method more than practicing scientists.[4] For instance, they were quicker to abandon hypotheses when the data didn't support them. The upshot is that objectivity is a property of the entire institution— the system—of science, extending over hundreds and even thousands of years; it is not, we repeat, a property of individual scientists.

If individual scientists were totally unbiased and completely objective, it would be a trivial matter to explain how and why the system of science is objective. The objectivity of science would follow directly from the objectivity of individual scientists. However, given that individual scientists *are* biased, it is much more interesting and important to understand that *the objectivity of the system emerges from the subjectivity of individual scientists.*

To summarize, in order to be objective, science must study itself with the same vigor and rigor with which it studies everything else on the earth and in the heavens above. This is the only way it can reveal and correct systematically and systemically its own flaws and defects. In short, it is only by being intensely self-reflective and self-critical that science or anything else can pretend to produce "objective truth."

INQUIRY SYSTEMS

To show what makes science such a powerful way of looking at the world, we look at it here from a special perspective, that of *inquiry systems*. An inquiry system is a particular way of obtaining knowledge about the world, but it is even more basic. Different inquiry systems differ fundamentally from one another in what they consider worthy of the term *knowledge*. That is, they have very different conceptions of knowledge and truth. Here we discuss five very different ways of producing knowledge—that is, five inquiry systems—and what they reveal about science.[5] In short, each inquiry system represents a different philosophical method and school for obtaining knowledge, or what it recognizes as knowledge in the first place.

A Prosaic Example

Because philosophy is such a difficult and daunting subject, in order to ground our discussion and make it as concrete and accessible as possible, we discuss the five archetypal ways of producing knowledge and truth in terms of a fictitious company, Healthy Bars, Incorporated. Healthy Bars is in fact an example we have used successfully with many different kinds of groups to explain the nature of philosophy and its relevancy to their careers and lives.

As its name indicates, Healthy Bars makes a variety of healthy-food energy bars. Its goal is not only to be the number one company in its industry in terms of market share, but also to be the company that consumers think of first when they think of an environmentally responsible and ethical company. To increase awareness of its products in order to boost sales, Healthy Bars decided to hold a worldwide contest. They invited consumers to send in recipes for "the perfect energy bar."[6] Consumers were free to use any ingredients they wished in their new bar, providing of course that the ingredients were safe, environmentally friendly, and legal. They were even free to modify any of Healthy Bars' current products. The contest winner would receive not only free energy bars for a year but, more important, the honorific title "master chef."

Although at first glance this example seems trite and far removed from science, we shall show shortly that it is anything but. Science is such a potent force and essential aspect of today's world that it has impacts on every aspect of modern life; indeed, every aspect of modern life makes use of science. Using a common example actually helps us to see this fact better than if we had used a more esoteric example. So, elements of science enter in throughout the Healthy Bars example. Indeed, it draws from both the applied physical and the social sciences.

The First Way of Producing Knowledge: Expert Consensus

As most organizations do, Healthy Bars appointed a small committee to judge the entries it received. To its chagrin, the committee soon found itself virtually drowning in entries. Thousands poured in from all over the world. It was completely stymied. There was no way that such a small group could sift through thousands of submissions.

Besides, what did *"perfect"* mean? They hadn't even considered that a definition of what they were looking for might be important before they started the contest. Rather naively, they had thought it would just emerge. (Recall from Chapter Two that only in exercises and well-structured problems do we start with a clear definition of the problem at the beginning of an inquiry. Further, the initial definition does not vary over the course of the inquiry.)

One of the committee members suggested tabulating all the entries by entering them into a computer. The recipe receiving the most votes or the one that had the most in common with all the other recipes—the "average"—would be declared the winner—the perfect fruit bar. The member pointed out that this was a convenient way of bypassing the definition of *perfect*, which would in effect emerge from the process itself. As another member of the committee said, "Why get hung up on definitions?"

However, as soon as this solution was suggested, it raised more concerns than it settled. Most of the committee members felt it was a complete copout. How was "average" in any sense the definition of *perfect*? Couldn't it lead to the selection of the most bland and inoffensive entry? Besides, what did it mean to "average" entries from around the world? Were all entries equal? Was everyone who submitted an entry an "expert"? Were all experts equal?

In effect, *the committee members couldn't agree to use the method of agreement to settle the contest!* Thus, this particular method was rejected before it even got started. (In other words, the taken-for-granted assumption that the problem was well-structured was false.)

Even if they polled "experts" for their opinions, there would be problems. For instance, how would they define *expert?* The committee felt that even if the experts were the community of distinguished chefs worldwide—say, all those working in two-star restaurants or better—having them choose the winner would be inadequate, for it would privilege a certain group of experts over all others. In using experts, one not only depends on the consensus between them to produce "truth" in the first place—truth in this case being the "perfect" fruit bar—but one also assumes that the more agreement there is between the experts, the stronger and therefore the better will be the "truth."[7] In this system, "truth" is that on which a group of experts agrees strongly.

Appropriately enough, this approach is known as the *expert consensus* way of producing knowledge, or way of knowing. "Truth" is the product of the agreement between the judgments, observations, or opinions of different experts.

In science, expert consensus takes the form of "tight agreement" among the data (facts, observations, and so on) produced by independent qualified experts and scientists. Take global warming as an example. The body of reputable scientists worldwide is now in substantial agreement that human activities are a significant factor responsible for global warming. This "fact" is taken as strong evidence that the debate over whether humans are or are not responsible for global warming is essentially over, even if all the mechanisms for it are not understood completely.

Agreement is no less important in science than in any field of human activity. One could in fact argue that agreement is even more important in science, because so much is riding on the outcomes of scientific knowledge.

The Second Way of Producing Knowledge: The One True Formula

One of the members on the committee had a bachelor's degree in chemistry from a top university. She argued that chemistry should be used to derive the ingredients and the recipe for the perfect fruit bar. The winner of the contest would be the person or persons whose submission matched the recipe derived from this procedure.

In the second inquiry system, the perfect recipe is based solely on the theoretical principles and laws of a "hard science," such as chemistry. Thus, in this system we see directly the linkage with science. Science is thus *the model* for inquiry, and truth is equivalent to a single formula.

The reasoning behind this model is that the perfect fruit bar—the "truth"—should not be based on anything so crass as the mere opinions of a group of experts, no matter how distinguished they may be. The assessment of truth shouldn't even be based on what a particular set of experts regard as the "facts," because the facts of one group and of one age have an uncanny way of becoming the falsehoods of another. After all, it was once a "fact" that the Earth was physically flat. That it is now socially "flat" is of course another matter.[8]

Truth should be based on the established principles—the laws—of hard science. In fact, by proceeding from firmly established scientific first principles, one should be able to derive a single formula. For instance, in the case of a falling body, the distance (D) it covers in a certain amount of time (T) is given by the familiar formula $D = (\frac{1}{2}) G T^2$, where G equals the acceleration due to gravity. This formula is familiar to those who have taken a basic course in physics. Because the formula for falling bodies can be derived directly from Newton's laws of gravitation—one of the first principles of physical science—the formula is akin to a hard law of nature. (Those who understand the differential calculus can derive it.) The important point is that this system seeks to produce a *single abstract formula* that it regards as "the truth."

Appropriately enough, this system is known as the *pure theory* way of knowing, which we refer to as the *One True Formula*.

This system is actually much broader and more basic than mathematics or science alone. The One True Formula is a coherent belief system—a framework of basic, presumably rational first principles. In this sense, it does not always appear as a formula.

Although he was probably unaware of it, Michael Kinsley, writing in *TIME* magazine, expressed the notion as follows:

Ideology is a good thing, not a bad one—and partisanship is at its worst when it is not about ideology. That's when it descends into trivia and slime. Ideology doesn't have to mean mindless intransigence or a refusal to accommodate new evidence or changing evidence. *It is just a framework of basic principles. A framework is more than a list: all the pieces should fit together [coherently].*[9]

Needless to say, the committee didn't buy this way of choosing the winner either. Why should the winner be decided by a single scientific discipline, let alone by something so ridiculous as a single formula? Why was chemistry superior to any other science or, for that matter, to any nonscientific discipline or profession, such as cooking? If one was restricted to choosing a single discipline, why shouldn't it be psychology? Weren't the attitudes of the contestants just as important as the physical ingredients themselves? (Shades of the Coca-Cola example in Chapter One.)

Because the committee couldn't answer their own questions based on their *own* first principles, they rejected the method of first principles in choosing the winner.

The Third Way of Producing Knowledge:
Multiple Perspectives or Formulas
One of the committee members suggested an approach that all of the members agreed with instantly. For the first time they felt they were making headway. (Notice that in agreeing so readily they were

buying into the first method, expert agreement. In effect, they were using the first way of producing knowledge to select another way of producing it. There is nothing inherently wrong with initially combining inquiry systems in order to select another method of reaching an important decision.[10] It is in fact an important way of getting around the weaknesses of any single system. The truth no longer depends on a single system.)

The suggestion was made that instead of lumping all of the entries together and averaging them, they could be grouped initially by countries or regions of the world; or they could be grouped first by schools or by philosophies of cooking. A winner could then be selected from each group by using the first way of producing knowledge, that is, by expert consensus.[11] Another way to put it would be to say that instead of there being a single, best formula for all of the entries, a different formula would be used to determine the winner of each group, and then an overall winner would be selected from among these.

The third inquiry system is a combination of the first two ways of producing knowledge—Expert Agreement and the One True Formula. In this approach, backed up by whatever data are available, the committee would look at how the recipes were created by the various regions or schools of cooking from which the recipes came. Presumably each region or school had used its own distinct formula for creating its recipe. This system would allow the committee members to witness how the outcome, the perfect fruit bar, varied as the underlying method or formula for producing the recipe changed. It would allow the committee members, who may not have been experts in or proponents of any particular school of cooking, to understand the reasoning behind each school's process by seeing how each approached the same problem.

This system allows its users to see explicitly the differences between various approaches. In other words, it does not leave variety to chance. Unlike the first two ways of producing knowledge, it does not reflect the belief that there is one best answer to a complex problem or question. To the contrary! *The third way is based in the belief that any problem of importance must be looked at from* at least two *different angles so that those who would address it can begin to ascertain whether they are committing Type Three and Type Four Errors.* Unless we have two or more formulations of a problem to consider, we cannot possibly know whether we are solving the "wrong" or the "right" problem. In fact, without two or more views to compare, the terms *right* and *wrong* have no meaning, unless of course one believes unequivocally that there is only one "truth" and one system or way of looking at the world. This system is thus a minimum requirement for determining whether Type Three and Type Four Errors are being committed.

The third way of knowing is also the basis of critical thinking. It forces one to examine the assumptions that underlie any particular formulation of a problem by explicitly comparing it with other formulations. After one has witnessed the differences between several approaches to or formulations of a problem, one can, if one wishes, pick and choose from among them, blending if need be, to form one's own unique recipe.

Appropriately enough, this system is known as the *Multiple Perspectives* or *Multiple Formulas* approach to knowledge. It argues that complex problems are too important to be left to the reasoning of a single approach, no matter how appealing it is. In fact, the more appealing a particular approach is, the more important it is to resist the temptation to fall exclusively under its sway. This system is also known as *multidisciplinary inquiry.* It results in a conclusion or recommendation that is the product of two or more scientific disciplines or professions. However, because the disciplines or professions involved in multidisciplinary inquiry are separate and not affected by one another, this system is not *inter*disciplinary. The disciplines and professions themselves do not change as a result of being involved in the third way of knowing. They remain unaffected. As we shall see, we have to reach the fifth system of producing knowledge, systems thinking, before we can say we are engaged in inquiry that is interdisciplinary.

Another, final aspect of this system is very important to note. The first two systems assume that data (expert judgments, facts, observations, and so on) and theory are independent of each other. Expert Consensus assumes that data and observations on an issue or phenomenon can be gathered without having to presuppose any prior theory. In other words, it assumes that data and observations are theory and value free. In contrast, the One Best Formula assumes that theories are free of data and observations, in that they depend on pure thought or logic alone. The third system, however, assumes that our prior beliefs, whether or not they take the form of the One True Formula, affect what we decide is important to collect or observe. Every observation we make presumes that we have made a decision about what is worth observing. This decision, and certainly the assumptions on which it is based, may be regarded as a form of theory, however informal it may be. In this sense, every observation presupposes prior theory. Data and observations are not theory free. They certainly are not value free.

The upshot is that through the notion of what is "worth observing," we have snuck ethics into the discussion. In other words, ethics are an important part of every inquiry, whether we acknowledge it or not. In fact, the less we acknowledge it, the more important it is, because the less we examine and debate our ethical assumptions, the more we take them for granted.

The Fourth Way of Producing Knowledge: Expert Disagreement

Someone on the committee had another idea. Instead of depending on the *agreement* between experts, suppose they used *dis*agreement. The winner of the debate between the experts would then be the winner of the contest. This approach is the direct opposite of the first approach. One of the most important and critical parts of an inquiry system is the *guarantor,* the part that "guarantees" that by starting with the "right" building blocks of knowledge—the basic assumptions, the elemental or fundamental "truths," the data and observations, and so on—and combining them in the "right" ways, one will arrive at "the truth." In the first approach to producing knowledge, consensus is the guarantor of the perfect fruit bar and of the way to produce it; in the fourth model, intense conflict is the guarantor.

In this approach, the committee members would pick the two schools of cooking that disagreed the most. They would then arrange a knockdown, no-holds-barred debate between them. The recipe that emerged from (survived) the debate, which might be neither of the original two recipes, would then be dubbed the "truth." This model is appropriately known as the *dialectical* theory or model of knowledge production. It is also known as the conflict theory of truth, or as *Expert Disagreement* for short.

To show how the fourth approach applies to business, and therefore in essence to all professions, consider the following tale. Alfred P. Sloan, chairman of General Motors from 1937 to 1956, was one of the few executives who not only understood the importance of the fourth way but actually used it when he had an important decision to make. When his top executives agreed too quickly and too readily with his ideas, Sloan said, it is reputed, "I propose we postpone further discussion until our next meeting to give ourselves time to develop disagreement and perhaps gain some understanding of what the decision is all about."[12]

A particularly instructive example of the fourth approach is the various definitions of death that are found in different cultures.[13] In the United States, death is defined by "brain death." This is partially because in the West the essence of a person—the self—is thought to lie in the brain, not in the body. The West thus subscribes to a *body-mind dualism* that dates back at least as far as Descartes. Another reason is that this criterion makes death relatively easy to determine. (In effect, it makes the determination of death into an exercise.) Only one organ has to fail in order to determine death (shades of the first two ways of knowing). When the brain "dies," the person dies as well, even though the body may not have died. By contrast, in Japan the person's soul is thought to reside in the body. Therefore, it is only when the body dies that the person has died.

These differences are not just matters of semantics. They have profound consequences for serious issues such as organ donation and transplantation, and thus for medical science in general. In the West, and in the United States in particular, organ transplantation is a huge business.[14] If death is defined as brain death and the body's organs can be kept viable through machines, then the body can be "harvested" for its remaining "parts." In the West brain death is quite commonly declared even when blood is still being pumped through the body by the heart, so all of the remaining organs are in some sense still alive. This certainly makes organ transplantation much more acceptable. In Japan, however, and in the East in general, a different definition of death and a different concept of the body make organ transplantation generally much less acceptable.

No wonder the differences between cultures are often so profound.

The Fifth Way of Producing Knowledge: Systems Thinking

The committee still wasn't satisfied. They still felt that something fundamental was missing, but they didn't know exactly what it was. Someone finally exclaimed, "We need help." Another person added, "We're thinking too narrowly. We need to expand our thinking." This led her to say, "Maybe we need to bring in someone who can help us to think more broadly. Isn't this what systems thinking is all about? Why don't we call in a systems expert?"

The fifth way of producing knowledge is the most comprehensive of all. It is known as the systems way of thinking, or simply as *Systems Thinking*. This model incorporates considerations that are typically overlooked in the first four models. For instance, ethical and aesthetic considerations are given center stage. Using the "right"—that is, ethical—ingredients (ones that are not harmful to the environment) is central to this approach. Another consideration is the ambience, that is, the aesthetic design, of the kitchen in which a fruit bar is produced, which is as important as the recipe itself. In fact, anything that affects the mental state and well-being of the cook—for example, the lighting and the color of the kitchen's walls—is potentially an essential part of the recipe.

This approach helped to put some of the entries in a special light (pun intended). A few of the entries described the setting in which the submission had been prepared. These entrants felt that the kitchen in which the fruit bars were prepared was as important as the raw ingredients themselves. For this reason, they included pictures of their kitchen along with their recipe.

THE ESSENCE OF SYSTEMS THINKING

The fifth way of knowing, Systems Thinking, is based on the work of C. West Churchman and his mentor, E. A. Singer Jr.[15] As we discussed in Chapter Six, Singer was one of William James's best students, and he emphasized that there are no "basic" disciplines. For both Singer and Churchman, no science, no profession or field of knowledge, was more basic or superior to any other. This idea is so important that it is one of the cornerstones of systems thinking.

In Systems Thinking, the physical sciences, which are certainly knowledge about the physical world, are inseparable from the social sciences and knowledge about the social world. (Recall the discussion in Chapter Six.) Churchman's philosophy, and that of his lifelong friend and colleague Russell Ackoff, is based on Singer's philosophy.[16] In their views, the physical and social sciences not only are inseparable but in fact presuppose each other. Neither is possible without the other. Again, whether we admit it or not, physical science is done by all-too-human beings who not only have a psychology but also operate within a social context. The psychology and sociology of the investigator affect not only the *production* of physical knowledge but also its very existence.[17] Indeed, that is what Mitroff's study of the Apollo moon scientists was all about.

THE RATIONALITY OF SCIENCE

One of Singer's most perceptive insights is relevant to our discussion of rationality and science. Although he lived long before neuroscientists discovered mirror neurons, Singer anticipated their discovery.[18] They were an integral part of his philosophy.

For Singer, there was no such thing as an isolated mind. The concept of mind was inherently social. Singer was fond of saying that it took at least two minds to have one. There was the *experiencing mind* and there was the *reflective mind*.

An isolated mind cannot determine whether it is making mistakes about its own mental states. One is hard put to observe oneself accurately, let alone objectively. The point is that we require other minds to determine whether we are committing Type Three or Type Four Errors. Don't we depend on others all the time to inform us of our true intentions? Don't others see things about us that we are unable and unwilling to see? Aren't the minds of others necessary for us to have a mind?

To get this point across, Singer used the seemingly simple example of a person in pain. When you are in pain, no one doubts that it is *your* pain, but it does not follow that the pain is solely yours. That is, just because the *primary physical and psychological experience* of pain is *yours*, the *knowledge* of it is not necessarily yours and yours alone.

Neuroscientists have shown convincingly that our brains are hardwired to "mirror" the emotions of others. Thus, if I am sad, then you feel sad to a certain extent as well. To a degree, all of us "feel your pain."[19]

But this was not Singer's main point. His main point was that we often aren't aware of our own pains until another person—another mind—points out our injuries. For instance, injuries are quite common in the heat of football games. It is also common for the person who has been injured not to feel any pain until play has stopped, his injury is pointed out, and he is helped off the field. Often it is only after these steps have occurred that the person feels pain.

For Singer, the *experiencing mind*—the person who broke his leg and was shortly to experience pain—was not the same as the *reflective mind*—the person witnessing the other person's injury. One person or mind had the primary experience—the injury—but another mind was necessary to help the first one know or interpret what he or she had experienced. The primary experience belonged to one mind, but the knowledge of it belonged to another.

The upshot of this discussion is that in order for science to be all it is cracked up to be, other minds are required to study science scientifically. Science needs to study itself with the same intensity that it pretends to study everything else under and beyond the sun. It needs to do this in order to see if it actually functions as it says it does, to keep itself honest.

There is, however, another twist. What is there to prevent a third mind from studying the first two, and so on ad infinitum? Nothing. If one experiencing mind needs another to keep it honest and informed, then doesn't the reflective mind need this as well? The answer is yes. (Historically, the biggest "other mind" has been God.)

A special combination of minds is pertinent to the conduct of science. This combination is especially overlooked and neglected by those who proclaim the superiority of rationality and science. In the case of the Apollo moon missions, the geological and physical scientists whom Mitroff was studying were the *primary minds* trying to make sense of the *primary objects* they were studying: the moon rocks. Mitroff was playing the role of the *secondary, reflective mind*. In this role, Mitroff was doing double duty. He was acting as both a social scientist and a philosopher of science.

One can literally shout to the heavens all day and all night long— that is, one can proclaim outright—that rationality and science are superior forms of knowing; but it is not until we actually study science scientifically and philosophically that we can begin to assure ourselves that they *are* in fact, or in conduct, superior. Claiming something doesn't make it so, as science is so fond of pointing out. When we actually do study science scientifically, we find that it is far more messy and complicated than is claimed by those who assert its superiority. It is filled with all kinds of irrational practices and beliefs.

Again, this doesn't mean that science is not a good way of knowing; it merely means that science is fundamentally dependent on philosophy, and in general on other fields of knowledge. By itself, science cannot make claims that apply to the entire universe. It is tied to philosophy and religion far more than it acknowledges (see the next chapter).

THE SUMMARY THUS FAR: OBJECTIVITY

Our discussion of different inquiry systems helps to make clear why the admonition to be objective is in most cases laughable, if not meaningless. Which *kind* of objectivity is the proper response?

According to the Expert Consensus model, something is objective if and only if it is based on hard data or observations, and on "tight agreement" between different observers. According to the One True Formula, something is objective if and only if it is based on logical reasoning from self-evident first principles. The trouble is that, as American humorist Ambrose Bierce observed, "self-evident means evident to one's self and to no one else."[20] According to the Multiple Perspectives method, something is objective if and only if it is the product of multiple points of view. According to the Expert Disagreement model, something is objective if and only if it is the product of (that is, only if it survives) the most intense debate between the most disparate points of view. Finally, in Systems Thinking, something is objective if and only if it is the product of the most intense effort of incorporating varied knowledge from the arts, humanities, professions, philosophy, sciences, and so on.

What, then, does it mean to be objective? It means to choose the "correct" mode of inquiry on the basis of the purposes of one's study; and to choose means to debate which mode of inquiry is "best" in the light of knowledge obtained through all of the various modes.

This same analysis applies to *right* and *wrong* with respect to problems, and hence to the Type Three and Type Four Errors. For example, according to Expert Consensus, something is "right" if and only if it is based on hard data or observations and when there is "tight agreement" between different observers; according to the One True Formula, something is "right" if and only if it is based on logical reasoning from self-evident premises; and so forth.

THE PROBLEM WITH SCIENCE

Traditional science primarily stresses only the first two inquiry systems or ways of producing knowledge (Expert Consensus and the One True Formula). Scientists pound into our minds well-accepted facts based on the first way of knowing, and they stress knowledge of well-accepted theories—the One Best Formula—in solving problems. Anything that cannot be reduced to hard data—the first way—or represented in terms of accepted theories—the second way—is false, misleading, and dangerous.

The first and second ways of producing knowledge are historically the foundations of education and of knowledge for a traditional "round world." However, they are seriously deficient and inadequate for a "flat world,"[21] that is, a world that is global and increasingly interconnected along every conceivable dimension—in short, a world composed of messes from top to bottom. For instance, they are too restrictive. They assume that the problems we need to solve are already well known and well defined. As we have stressed throughout, however, the problem with most problems is how to define what the problem is in the first place. For this reason, the Type Three and Type Four Errors are part and parcel of every problem that is important.

The first two ways are not well suited for complex problems. For instance, the world is undergoing a financial crisis not seen since the Great Depression. Surely the definition, let alone the resolution, of the crisis is as difficult and as messy as the Iraq war. This is precisely where the third (Multiple Formulas), fourth (Expert Disagreement), and fifth (Systems Thinking) ways of producing knowledge are required. The third way, Multiple Formulas or Perspectives, says that we need to see multiple definitions of a problem so that we can even attempt to avoid Type Three Errors. Again, how can we even begin to assess, let alone know, if we are solving the "wrong" problem if we don't have more than one formulation of the problem to consider? We can't. Comparing two or more formulations of a problem is no iron-clad guarantee that we will solve the right problems precisely. At best, it is a minimal guarantor. We can say, however, that without examining two or more formulations, the probability of committing Type Three and Type Four Errors goes up considerably.

The third, fourth, and fifth ways of knowing require us to exercise judgment, and an even more precious commodity: wisdom.

We have to decide which problems, in our best judgment, can be solved, resolved, dissolved, or absolved.

THE MORAL

The moral of the story is *not* that we should never use the first two ways of knowing but that we should use them only after we have assured ourselves that after using the third, fourth, and fifth ways we are working on the right problem to begin with. The third, fourth, and fifth ways are best suited for problem formulation; the first two ways are best suited for problem solving, once we are certain that we have defined the problem correctly.

A complex, globally interconnected world requires that we *manage* problems—messes—not solve them as we attempted to do in a simpler, fragmented world. A complex, globally interconnected world also requires that we acknowledge that the predominant philosophical bases of the simpler, fragmented world—the first two ways of knowing—no longer apply in their entirety. They apply only in the sense that we still collect data when we can and we still apply accepted scientific thinking, but we accept the limitations of these methods.

In the end, one of the essential aspects of Systems Thinking is the realization that we get out of inquiry only what we put into it initially; and what we put into every inquiry, fundamentally, is "us," through our collective psychology.

In far too many cases we are obsessed with what John Dewey referred to as "the quest for certainty."[22] The first two ways of producing knowledge differ only in where they locate the certainty we so desperately seek. The first way, Expert Consensus, attempts to find certainty in hard data and agreement among experts—supposedly the indubitable "facts" on which everyone can agree. The second way, the One Best Formula, attempts to find it in the indisputable scientific laws of nature, pure thought, or abstract logic. For Dewey, both approaches were neurotic attempts on the part of humankind to manage the anxiety brought about by the dangerous and uncertain world into which all of us are born. Notice that Dewey did not say that basic facts or elemental truths were neurotic in themselves. What was neurotic was our obsessive need for certainty. The danger is not that we will agree but that we will agree too readily because of being pressured to go along with the crowd.

The words of noted political columnist E. J. Dionne Jr. provide a fitting conclusion to the discussion thus far:

> Honest to goodness, I truly prefer consensus, civility, and problem solving. But if there is one thing worse than the absence of bipartisanship, it is a phony and ultimately unstable [first way] consensus that sells out everybody's [second way] principles. For better or worse, we have a lot of fighting and arguing [the fourth way] to do before we can enter the gates of a truly bipartisanship paradise.[23]

CONCLUDING REMARKS: A POSTSCRIPT ON BUSINESS EDUCATION

The contents of this chapter apply far beyond science as traditionally defined. Indeed, they apply to every branch of knowledge and profession. This is especially the case in today's world, because more and more branches of knowledge aspire to be "scientific." In particular, this chapter is relevant to many of the issues of education with which we dealt in Chapter Five, but we had to wait to explore them until we had discussed the inquiry systems in this chapter.

In the 1960s, two distinguished Columbia University professors, Robert A. Gordon and James Howell, produced a devastating critique of the state of business school education at the time. Known widely as the Gordon-Howell report, it criticized business education as sloppy, vague, imprecise, qualitative, lacking in rigor, and so on.[24] In other words, business school education hadn't even reached the levels of the first two forms of inquiry, that is, Expert Consensus and the One True Formula.

The Gordon-Howell report recommended that people be hired immediately from the social sciences and related disciplines to beef up business education. In effect, the basic recommendation was that business education needed to be based on a solid foundation of science. As a result, newly minted PhDs, primarily from the social sciences and engineering, came into business schools in droves. (Mitroff was one of the first to came in from the "outside"—in his case, from industrial engineering and the philosophy of social science.) Within a few decades, they radically transformed business schools so that they were seen as legitimate purveyors of knowledge by their counterpoints in the hard sciences. In short, Expert Consensus and the One True Formula were brought in to revolutionize business school education from top to bottom.

Little did business schools know at the time that by succeeding with very narrow criteria they were, in the words of Peter Drucker, sowing the seeds for the future "failure of success." By becoming hard-nosed, by elevating quantitative research (inquiry systems one and two) over qualitative, by stressing publications in so-called A-level academic journals over publications for practitioners, and by reproducing "scholars" who were as narrowly trained as they were instead of continuing to bring in people from the outside, they failed to see that they were setting themselves up for a new and even worse crisis. They attained precision, rigor, and respectability at the expense of relevance and, most of all, the ability to tackle complex problems, that is, messes. They failed by succeeding along very narrow grounds. Although they didn't know it, they were the vanguard for business education for a round world. Above all, they certainly didn't know that such an education is the worst preparation of all for what *New York Times* bestselling author Thomas Friedman has called (as mentioned in the previous chapter) a "flat world."[25]

In short, they were the perfect prescription for committing Type Four Errors.

8 ORGANIZED RELIGION
Misconstruing God

God's revelation had been a gradual, evolutionary process; at each stage of their history. [H]e had adapted [H]is truth to the limited capacity of human beings. The teaching and guidance that God had given to Israel had changed over time. The religion entrusted to Abraham was tailored to the needs of a simpler society than the Torah bestowed on Moses or David.[1]

THE BY-PRODUCTS OF A LONG-GONE AGE

Both religious fundamentalists and the so-called new atheists, such as Sam Harris, Richard Dawkins, and Christopher Hitchens, seriously misconstrue the nature of God.[2] Atheists, or "scientific fundamentalists," as Chris Hedges labels them, vehemently deny the existence of God, and hence also deny that God has any properties that are inherently good and beneficial for humankind. Religious fundamentalists generally argue for an outmoded conception of God that is rooted in the social conditions, problems, and tribalism's of some five thousand years ago. This God is mean, petty, vindictive, and violent. He is a quintessentially old-time, old-fashioned, "take no prisoners," masculine warrior God.

Karen Armstrong has pointed out masterfully that the major religions of the world are the products of a long-gone Axial Age.[3] They are the "solutions" to the economic, social, and spiritual problems of five thousand years. They don't necessarily work—and certainly not completely—as solutions to today's problems. Instead of continuing to solve the problems of a bygone age, and hence committing Type Three and Type Four Errors in the name of religion, we need new conceptions of God that are better suited to the problems of our times.

For the great rationalist philosophers of the seventeenth century (Descartes, Leibniz, Spinoza), God was inherently necessary. God was the Guarantor of Our Decisions (G.O.D.). God kept us from erring in reaching important conclusions and making important decisions. In other words, God was the keeper or guarantor of reason. Although the G.O.D. of the seventeenth century may no longer apply to our times, what form, if any, does work for us, and is needed to avoid (as much as is humanly possible) Type Three and Type Four Errors?

NO TOPIC IS MORE DIFFICULT, MORE BASIC, AND MORE PERSISTENT

No topic is more difficult or more treacherous to discuss than God, religion, and spirituality. Yet no topic is more basic, more important, and more central to the human condition. Try as we might, God, religion, and spirituality will not go away. God, religion, and spirituality not only deal with but are an expression of *ultimate concern*—our inborn preoccupation with ultimate matters. For this reason alone we would be seriously remiss if we failed to talk about them, especially in a book that pretends to discuss some of humankind's most fundamental problems and the errors that result from our attempts and flawed solutions to them.

In spite of the contentions of the new atheists, it is far from clear that religion is the wrong solution to the wrong problem. It is also not clear that it is irrational to believe in God or to practice religion, and it is far from having been proved that religion is the scourge of humankind and that therefore we would all be better off without it.[4]

Even if all religion were suddenly to vanish from the face of the planet, it is naive to believe that the human needs and passions that give rise to it would vanish as well. Some other facet of the human condition would merely replace religion. To see religion as the source of all human problems is as misguided as seeing history, politics, or sociology as the source of all evil in the world.[5]

Worst of all, science would also vanish, because, as we argued in previous chapters, the same human needs and passions are present in science as well. These needs and passions motivate all scientists, great and not so great.

VARYING CONCEPTIONS

It is certainly not the case that our conceptions of God, religion, and spirituality have been fixed and unchanging over the course of human history, development, and evolution. To the contrary, they have changed dramatically, a fact that atheists are prone to overlook. To reject the conception of God at one point in human history is not to reject it at all points in time.[6]

God, religion, and spirituality have been viewed variously as arising out of and as expressions of humankind's

1. deep-seated fear and ignorance of the unknown and of death in particular; that these fears are so deep and the consequences of believing in the "wrong" God are so great accounts for the constant wars and power struggles over religion, especially over who controls access to heaven and God (Hobbes[7]), and societies' deep-seated aggression and tribal hatreds (see the Old Testament).

2. inherent need to address ultimate concerns, to provide hope, and to resolve the constant search for meaning and purpose (as in the great religions of the Axial Age).

3. constant need for falsehoods and illusions to bear the brunt of the harshness of life and the fear of death; from this perspective, religion is a "royal delusion" (see Plato, Marx, and Freud).

4. intense need to belong to a special and favored community (Israel of the Old Testament).

5. deep-seated communal and social nature and the "fact" that we are part of nature itself, which in its original state was uncorrupted and good (see Rousseau).

6. deep-seated and persistent need for a guarantor for certainty, knowledge, and truth (see Descartes, Leibniz, and Spinoza).

7. need for a firm philosophical foundation and justification for ethics, hope, and salvation (see Kant).

8. belief in the manifestation of Spirit working its way and developing through the state as the highest expression of civilization (see Hegel).

9. belief in the manifestation of Spirit as the expression of the cosmos, that is, the universe itself (see Ken Wilber).[8]

This is of course only a tiny sampling of the many and diverse conceptions of God, religion, and spirituality that humankind has developed. Nonetheless, even this short list is enough to demonstrate that as humankind has developed and evolved, so has its conceptions of God, religion, and spirituality. This is true not only for the religions of the West, but also for those of the East.[9]

BASIC QUESTIONS AND ISSUES

In this chapter we discuss the following broad questions and issues. Each is central to our appraisal of what, if any, Type Three and Type Four Errors have been committed in the name of religion:

1. Does God exist?

2. If so, what are God's properties? That is, what is God like?

3. How can we reconcile the notion of a loving God with the enormous amount and the kinds of evil that exist in the world?

4. Can it be proved conclusively beyond all doubt that God positively exists? (This question is of course related to the first question in this list. Obviously if God does not exist, then God does not have any properties, except nonexistence. Nonetheless, one can talk about the properties of God whether God exists or not.

Furthermore, because the history of human thought has tended to separate the two questions, we have as well.)

5. Conversely, can it be proved conclusively that God does *not* exist?

6. What are the various stages of human development and evolution?

7. To what stages of human development and evolution do the various images and conceptions of God correspond, and why?

THE SPIRIT OF DEVELOPMENT
AND THE DEVELOPMENT OF SPIRIT

Because they are so fundamental to our entire discussion, we begin with the last two items on the preceding list of questions. We primarily discuss a particular theory of human development and evolution.

Because the whole subject is invariably controversial, some important qualifications are in order. First, we are not claiming that there is one and only one theory of human development and spirituality. Such a claim would be preposterous. However, we need some theory of human development and spirituality if we are even to identify the various levels or stages of being, let alone support the admittedly controversial claim that some stages are higher or lower than others. (The idea that we need "some theory" follows directly from the third inquiry system, multiple perspectives, discussed in the last chapter. We need some theory if we are to identify *any*thing as a *some*thing, let alone as stages or levels.)

Second, we are also not claiming that Western modes or theories of human development are superior to Eastern ones, or vice versa. We are certainly not proposing a "clash of civilizations" in which some civilizations are supposedly superior to others. We believe nothing of the sort. Thus, we need a theory of human development and spirituality that does equal justice to the East and the West.

At a minimum, we are saying that different levels or stages of human development can indeed be clearly identified. These stages can be sharply differentiated from one another. That is, the characteristics and properties of one stage are markedly distinct from those of other stages. In addition, we are also claiming that every civilization has individuals who are at different stages of development. For this reason, it is not correct to lump together individuals who are at different stages and then claim that some civilizations in their entirety are superior to others.

The strongest claim is of course that some stages are "higher" than others in the chain of human development and evolution. This claim does not necessarily imply a strict hierarchy, a concept that is highly offensive to many.[10] However, it does imply that some individuals are more highly developed along certain lines than others. At the same time, it also implies that everyone is more developed along certain lines than everyone else.

The least controversial claim is that every stage has desirable aspects. The most controversial is that some aspects of every stage are "higher" than each of the stages that precede it. Those who disagree with ideas about hierarchy, stages, or higher or lower levels are often guilty of asserting exactly what they do not like in others, but in a more surreptitious fashion. In effect, they are saying that their way of thinking—the standpoint that rejects all hierarchies—is "better than" or "superior" to other positions. In saying this, they have just asserted a hierarchy. This is similar to the position of those postmodernists who claim that all positions are equally valid, except of course their own, which is superior to others. A deeper response is that pro-hierarchy and anti-hierarchy views are dialectically related. (See the fourth inquiry system, Expert Disagreement, discussed in the last chapter.) They are "dialectical twins," so to speak. Both pro-hierarchy and anti-hierarchy views are fundamentally dependent on the other for their existence and meaning. Because one view is always being compared and contrasted with the other, one can't be defined without the other. Conversely, the existence of one implies the other. For this reason, although we don't necessarily agree completely with the notion of hierarchy, we don't disagree completely with it either. Indeed, the inclusion of hierarchy makes discussion of the different stages of human development as forceful, clear, and sharp as possible.

We would also add that not all hierarchies are inherently and necessarily bad. They are certainly not all equal. The fact that the method of knowledge referred to in the last chapter as Systems Thinking argued that there is not a hierarchy among different fields of knowledge does not mean there are no valid hierarchies at all for other needs and purposes.

AN INTEGRAL PHILOSOPHY: PART ONE

Although he is by no means the only person who has written extensively on human development, Ken Wilber's *integral philosophy* is one of the most important and comprehensive theories to date. It is also one of the clearest ways to grasp the nature of human development.[11] It not only embraces Eastern and Western forms equally, but also integrates them into a comprehensive whole.

Like most theorists of human development, Wilber is basically concerned with identifying different psychological ways of being in relation to the world.[12] He starts by noting that there are two dimensions that differentiate a person's orientation to the world: (1) inner versus outer, that is, whether one is tuned primarily to one's thoughts and feelings or to the external world; and (2) the individual versus the group, that is, whether the unit of analysis with which one thinks about problems is the individual or the group; for instance, in Chapter Five we talked about how for Judge Judy all problems are personal and individual, not social or institutional. Combining the ends of the two dimensions in all possible ways results in four distinct orientations, or quadrants: inner individual, inner group, outer individual, and outer group.

Inner refers to all aspects of a person or society that are internal, such as thoughts and emotions. *Outer* refers to all aspects that are external, such as actions, biological conditions, physical structures, and so on.

Recall from Chapter Two that conservatives tend to blame the poor for not having the "right" internal beliefs to allow them to work their way out of poverty entirely on their own, while liberals, on the other hand, blame external institutions for not providing the "right" kinds of support to help the poor get out of poverty. Thus Wilber's model can be used in spheres other than the spiritual.

The *inner-individual orientation* has to do with all of the thoughts and emotions of a single person—in general, their internal conscious and unconscious states of mind. The *inner-group orientation* has to do with societies, cultures, civilizations, institutions, organizations—the shared experiences, thoughts, and feelings of two or more individuals. The *outer-individual orientation* relates to the external structure of a person, that is, to a person's physical body, fitness, and health. The *outer-group orientation* is concerned with the external structures of an organization, institution, society, and so on.

Consider a simple example.

It is well known that different cultures view space and time very differently. For instance, the distance that people stand apart from each other when talking varies enormously. In Anglo-European cultures people stand farther apart than they do in Latin and non-European cultures.[13] The outer-individual aspect in this case would be the actual physical distance between and body positions of the individuals engaging with each other. The inner-individual aspect would be how comfortable, for instance, a person feels when another person is close to or far from him or her. The outer-group aspect is how space is shared and used in different cultures. The inner-group aspect is the attitudes that different cultures have about physical and psychological space.

Now let's look at a more difficult concept: spirituality.[14]

Throughout history there have been at least four very different notions of spirituality. The outer-individual notion reflects the view that the human body is such a wondrous mechanism that it is a manifestation of the Divine. The inner-individual notion considers all of the intense emotions and other psychological states that accompany spiritual and religious experience such as contemplating the mystery and the wonder of the universe. For many people, these inner states *are themselves* the Divine. The outer-group notion refers to the organizational structures of religious institutions; for example, for its members the Catholic Church itself is a manifestation of the Divine. Finally, the inner-group notion considers the shared emotions and other psychological states that people experience when they participate in group religious or spiritual settings. For instance, it is well known that trances are often easily induced in such situations. None of these orientations is more fundamental than any of the others. Indeed, they all depend on one another. Although we can distinguish between them, and thus give them separate labels, they are inseparable.

Let's take another example: the environment. Many people in the environmental movement regard as fundamental the outer-group orientation, which sees nature itself in deity-like terms. (This is one of the historic forms of spirituality; it views all of nature—that is, the entire universe—as a manifestation of the Divine.) However, in order to respect the environment and treat it ethically, all four orientations are required. Profound internal changes are required in how individuals (inner-individual) and organizations and governments (inner-group), for example, view—that is, feel and think about— the environment if they really want to do something positive, such as counteract global warming. Outer-individual changes, such as in the kinds of cars individuals drive, are also required.

Finally, individuals, organizations, and whole societies can be at different levels of development in whatever orientation they are primarily situated. This idea results in one of the most succinct expressions of Wilber's integral philosophy:

All levels; all quadrants.

All quadrants; all levels.[15]

The basic idea is that regardless of the level of development a person has attained *within* a particular quadrant, he or she should strive to incorporate *all* of the remaining quadrants. In addition, regardless of which quadrant a person is in, he or she should strive to reach an even higher level of development within that quadrant. The reason a person should strive to incorporate all of the quadrants is in order to be well balanced, that is, to be equally developed along all dimensions. To be able to see all problems from at least four points of view is a minimal guarantor of completeness, that one is solving the "right problem" and therefore avoiding Type Three and Type Four Errors. In short, all four quadrants are needed both to raise and to answer complex questions about the human condition. Another way to put it is as follows: *One of the fundamental forms of the Type Three and Type Four Errors occurs when we take, and thereby mistake, one or two quadrants for all of them. This occurs when we take, and thereby mistake, our preferred psychological form of reality for the whole of reality. In short, we elevate our preferred way of looking at the world over all other ways of looking at it.*

As Wilber stresses repeatedly, one cannot overemphasize the difficulties that the preceding concept poses. For instance, ever since the rise of modern science, the inner-individual quadrant has been steadily under attack. In effect, modern science ridicules and therefore dismisses anything that cannot be reduced to the outer-individual. In other words, it dismisses any phenomena that cannot be studied by, and thereby reduced to, hard observations (Expert Consensus) and theory (the One Best Formula).

What both modern science and the humanities have great difficulty understanding, and thereby accepting, is not only that there are methods for studying the inner-individual (for example, through personal meditation and phenomenology) but, even more fundamental, that to dismiss the inner-individual quadrant all together is in effect to dismiss the core of what makes us human, that is, our deepest thoughts and emotions. Indeed, one can always ask, What does a person feel when he or she dismisses his or her feelings? And what does a group or society "feel" when it denigrates its "feelings"?[16]

To expand on the preceding point, in the last chapter we showed, although not in the same terms, that if we ruled out the inner-individual quadrant altogether, then modern science would also cease to exist. Scientists have, and have to have, immense feelings about their creations. Their feelings cause them, rightly and wrongly, to defend their pet theories and hypotheses rationally and irrationally. It they didn't, their pet creations would die untimely and premature deaths. In short, science is done by human, all-too-human, beings.

AN INTEGRAL PHILOSOPHY: PART TWO—
STAGES OF HUMAN DEVELOPMENT

The second part of Wilber's theory of human development is based on the work of Claire Graves and, more recently, Don Beck's work on Spiral Dynamics.[17] It is also based on the ideas of many other leading social scientists, such as the late Harvard developmental psychologist Lawrence Kohlberg.

The basic idea is that, as far as we know, humankind has developed and can potentially develop through a limited number of stages—we have identified nine here. These stages are not only developmental but also historical. Most important and fundamental, however, is that they are *states of mind,* that is, attitudes toward the world.[18]

1. Inert matter

2. Animal

3. Magic

4. Tribal

5. City-state

6. Nation-state

7. Super nation-state

8. Green

9. Kosmic

These stages are primarily for the outer-group quadrant. There are corresponding stages for the rest of Wilber's quadrants as well. However, to make discussion of an inordinately difficult topic easier, we have restricted ourselves to the preceding stages.

Inert Matter

Inert matter is the primeval, chemical stuff out of which life evolved. Although most of us don't think of it as such, this initial stage is best conceived of as the chemical imprint of the cosmos or universe. This stage represents the physical and chemical basis for life. At this level, all there is, is bare, inert, material existence. There is no kind of consciousness whatsoever. Inert matter exhibits function, but not human purpose. Whatever purpose exists is cosmic or divine.

As physical creatures we are built out of matter and thus carry the "residue" of matter in our cells. At the same time, we are also much more than matter alone.

Animal

The second stage is the bare beginnings of human consciousness. Creatures at the animal stage are still governed mostly by blind instincts—hence the term *animal*. Nonetheless, there are glimmerings of the animal's recognition of its separateness, uniqueness, and even "mind."

The bare beginnings of God, religion, and spirituality are also found at this stage. God is worshiped in the form of various animals because God is viewed as literally an animal. If we go back thousands of years, we see clear evidence of the struggle for the emergence of human consciousness from this animal stage in the myriad art forms that show half human, half animal creatures, such as minotaurs.[19] For this reason, Wilber refers to this as the minotaur stage of human development. Images of half human, half animal creatures show that humans are still not completely separated from their animal origins. They still identify strongly with the animal side of their psyches.

Magical

The next stage is the stage in which humans attribute magic to the "spirits" in animals, trees, forests, and so on. They not only accredit spirits with being there, but they literally hear and see them. Thus these spirits are real to them. Even today we find people who believe in such spirits. Indeed, they use their beliefs to induce trancelike states in themselves and in others.

The God, or gods, of this stage can be male, female, or some combination of the two, that is, androgynous.

Tribal

The tribal stage is when humans began to form communities organized for the purpose of gathering food, hunting, and later for growing food. Such as they were, tribes helped to ensure survival. The tribal stage is also when humans began to organize along lines that reflected their shared beliefs in various deities. As a result, different tribes worshiped different gods and fought one another over territory and beliefs.[20]

The archetypal God of this stage is the God of the Old Testament. He is a predominantly masculine, angry, vengeful, awe- and fear-inspiring God. He not only keeps his distance from humans, but also treats them like children. Depending on his moods, he can even treat them like favored children, as he did with Israel.

The gods of this stage are also referred to as *mythic*. In this stage we find gods who assume human or personal form, for example, Jesus of the New Testament.

City-State

At the city-state level of human development, for the first time people began to organize themselves into communities that cut across tribal lines. The emergence of the city-state was a landmark stage of human evolution.[21]

Nation-State

The nation-state stage includes not only the formation of the modern nation-state but also the Enlightenment and all of its accomplishments, the most notable of which were the emergence of reason and the separation of religion, science, and politics. For the first time, science was free from the constraints of religion and politics.

At this level of development we find two opposing and contradictory views of God and religion. At the one pole we find Thomas Hobbes. At the opposite end we find Jean-Jacques Rousseau. At the Hobbesian end of the spectrum, God and religion are responses to humanity's instinctive fear of nature and himself, of his untamed and brutish nature. God is to be feared because God is man's projection outward of his inner fearful nature onto the universe itself. At the other end of the spectrum is Rousseau, who sees God and religion as not to be feared but to be embraced. God and religion are responses to man's inherently social nature, to his instinctive desire to exist in a cooperative state with his fellow men.

The Enlightenment also brought us the philosophical gods of Descartes, Leibniz, Spinoza, Kant, and Hegel. The movement was from God as supreme guarantor of certain knowledge and truth (Descartes, Leibniz, Spinoza, and Kant), to God as a necessary postulate for the attainment of an ethical life (Kant), to God as the supreme expression of the human spirit working its way through and being the product of civilization (Hegel).

The Super Nation-State

The modern "super nation-state" began to emerge in the eighteenth and nineteenth centuries. It represents not only the emergence but also the dominance of a few megapowers. Although *dominance* is defined mainly in terms of material means and military power, it is also measured in the sophistication of social institutions and the strength of societal values.[22]

The modern super nation-state represents the philosophy and values of what Thomas Friedman has referred to as a "round world,"[23] that is, a world of distinct political entities separated widely in space and time. In spite of bodies such as the United Nations that represent humankind's attempts to manage the world as a whole, megastates (for example, the European Union) and increasingly corporations are the primary means of organizing the world order. Borders are still sacrosanct even though crisis problems such as global warming, finance, pollution, and terrorism are global, that is, messy and systemic.

The gods of this stage seem to be a return to the antagonistic and tribal gods of thousands of years ago. Some have gone so far as to characterize this stage as a primal "clash of civilizations." Indeed, both terrorists and some fundamentalists not only embrace mythic conceptions of God but are prepared to use the advanced technologies of modern societies to kill those who do not share their views.

In effect, they want to use modern technology to return all of us to premodern states.

Although these stages generally reflect a progression from less advanced to more advanced, from lower to higher, it is not impossible for them to co-exist, and furthermore there is no guarantee that we won't regress to earlier stages.

Green

The green stage is a new and different state, or plane, of human awareness. Not only are traditional national boundaries increasingly irrelevant, but they are also dangerous. Traditional boundaries and national identities keep us from respecting and managing the planet as a whole. Problems need not only to be formulated and reformulated in terms of the Earth as a whole, but also to be managed in terms of the whole.

Not only is the green stage a new level of human consciousness, but it also embraces a new conception of God, one that is neither masculine nor feminine. It is a universal, more "spiritual" conception that attempts to rise above the old tribal gods that have divided humankind since the beginning of time itself. In the age and spirit of environmentalism, it is an image of God that embraces and symbolizes the need for humans to change fundamentally their orientation to themselves and to the entire planet.[24]

Kosmic

Finally, the Kosmic stage (which for Wilber is not the same as Cosmos, that is, the physical universe) manifests humankind's spiritual connection with the entire universe. In this stage, the universe is experienced solely in spiritual terms. It is itself a spiritual being. In sum, the term *Kosmic* differentiates the spiritual universe from the physical universe, that is, the Cosmos.

Presumably only the most spiritually enlightened people have attained this last stage of development. At this level, the person and the universe are perceived as one. Because the individual has merged, as it were, with the entire universe, there is an overpowering sense of oneness. As a result, all distinctions and dichotomies—such as the individual versus the group, objective versus subjective, facts versus values—vanish.

THE TYPE THREE AND FOUR ERRORS

As we progress through the various stages there is an expanding sense of self, purpose, and group identity, and the corresponding vanishing of tribal and national identities. We become part of larger and larger wholes. Also, each successive stage incorporates each of the preceding ones.

To say that this makes for certain challenges is putting it mildly. Those who presumably are at higher stages can understand and communicate (often with great difficulty) with those at lower stages, but not the other way around. They speak totally different psychological-stage languages, as it were.

Although Wilber certainly hasn't used our concepts and words, his theory gives rise to an interesting formulation of the Type Three and Type Four Errors. These errors are due primarily to our fundamental failure to appreciate that the basic conceptions of God, religion, and spirituality that are appropriate to—and natural consequences of—lower stages of development are not appropriate for higher stages. That is, *we commit Type Three and Four Errors when we attempt to solve the problems of higher stages, such as the management of the planet as a whole, with the concepts and tools of lower stages.* In fact, we contend that *problems cannot be solved at the stages in which they are presented. They must be formulated and solved at higher stages.*

ARGUMENTS FOR THE EXISTENCE OF GOD

Arguments for and against the existence of God, and about what God's properties are, parallel somewhat the developmental theory we have been examining. The very earliest stages of development do not consist of formal, deductive arguments for the existence of God but of the felt, direct experience of the presence of God. Even today this is the primary mode by which most people apprehend and experience God—not through the dispassionate intellect but through the passions and emotions. This way of apprehending God is not necessarily irrational.

St. Anselm of Canterbury (1033–1109) was among the first to give a so-called logical proof for the existence of God.[25] The fact that his argument fails, and continues to fail despite the admirable and ingenious efforts of modern philosophers to rescue it by repairing its deficiencies,[26] does not make it less important. St. Anselm's argument demonstrates that although it is currently impossible (and may be forever) to give airtight, logically and definitively conclusive arguments *for* the existence of God, it is also impossible to give airtight, logically and definitively conclusive arguments *against* the existence of God. In effect, the One Best Formula way of thinking, or pure rationalism, fails when it comes to proving the existence or nonexistence of God.

Trying to establish by purely logical proofs the existence or nonexistence of God may be the supreme example of trying to prove propositions that are undecideable by formal methods alone (see the second inquiry system, the One True Formula, discussed in the last chapter). In either case, we are required to know too much about the universe. When it comes to formal proofs, the deist, theist, and atheist are equally on shaky grounds.

For purposes of brevity, we paraphrase St. Anselm's argument as follows: *Even the fool recognizes that God is the very Being than which one cannot imagine that there exists an even greater Being. Obviously a Being that exists is greater than One that does not. Therefore, God exists.* Or consider this version: *By definition, God is the most perfect Being imaginable. Now, a Being that exists is more perfect than One that does not exist. That is, an existing Being contains more of the attributes of perfection than One that does not exist. Therefore, God exists.*

The great philosopher Immanuel Kant was among the first to see through this line of argument and to point out its flaws. Suppose we imagine a chair and we list all its properties: it's brown, of a certain size, value, location, shape, and so on. Now, the "fact" that the chair "exists" is not the same as saying that it is brown, and so on. For if we take away the chair's existence, then we take away all of its other properties simultaneously. In short, existence is not an attribute or a property like brown, and so on. According to Kant, the attempt to establish the existence of a thing from its definition alone is thus fundamentally flawed.

Nonetheless, according to modern philosophers, Kant may have been wrong.[27] In mathematics, for example, there are cases in which we do establish the existence of things on the basis of their definition. Thus, the case may not be as clear-cut as previously thought. If the existence of mathematical entities can follow from their definition, then why would this not apply to supposedly "greater" things such as God?

More to the point, what does *perfection* mean? As with most things human, an almost infinite number of meanings and interpretations can be given to every word and human symbol. For this reason, the original authors and interpreters of the Bible were extremely wary of written versions—which tended to concretize, and corrupt, meanings and definitions—and strongly preferred oral interpretations.[28] Another reason is that many have felt that it is entirely inappropriate to apply human properties and terms—that is, human language—such as *existence,* to God. Whatever God "is," God is beyond human terms. However, by saying that God is beyond human terms we are using human terms! Thus, if God is anything, God is paradoxical.

The upshot of this discussion is that pure, formal, logical proofs for and against the existence of God may well be the wrong solutions to the wrong problems. After all, do purely formal proofs help us to lead better lives?

METAPHYSICAL ARGUMENTS

The preceding discussion is not to say that there are no compelling arguments for the existence of God. The argument that has the most appeal for us is as follows: Science alone cannot establish that the universe is both orderly and intelligible, or comprehensible and understandable by humans. Instead, science has to assume the basic orderliness, not to mention continuity, and intelligibility of the universe so that science is even possible. Historically these assumptions are due to religion.[29] Without them, science could not even get off the ground. That is, science is not possible without them. But these and other basic assumptions cannot be proven. Indeed, one has to assume them in constructing anything that even resembles a proof. They are basic metaphysical assumptions about the nature of reality. The name we give for both the nature and the existence of these assumptions is none other than God.

Another argument is as follows: The great theoretical physicist Stephen Hawking once raised the following question: Suppose one day physicists are finally able to write down the equations for everything, that is, all of physical reality. Nonetheless, even then one will still be able to ask, *What was it that breathed life into the equations? What made them come to life?* In our language, *What was it that* implemented *the equations?* The name we give is God.

The trouble with both of these responses is that in the first case God is nothing more than the Grand Metaphysician, the Big Philosopher in the Sky. In the second case, God is nothing more than the Grand Implementer. Neither characterization is sufficient to inspire the common person to acts of greatness. Perhaps the best that can be said is that they also do not inspire the ordinary person to commit grand acts of evil—but we wouldn't bet on it.

THE EXISTENCE OF EVIL

Of all the questions and issues pertaining to God, religion, and spirituality, none is more perplexing and ultimately unsatisfying than the question of evil. If God is supposed to be all loving, then how can God "allow"—if that is the "right" way to put it—so much evil in the world? The traditional response is that God could of course have made a world in which there was no evil at all, only good; but such a world would reduce us, in effect, to automatons. We would have no free will or choice because there would be nothing from which to choose. In giving us maximal freedom, God gave us the freedom to choose between good and evil—the ultimate choice, as it were. For choice to be meaningful, it has to be both real and significant. The desire to remove evil is the ultimate attention-getter and motivator of humans. There are other responses: If we had the mind of God, then we could see the purposes of both good and evil. From the standpoint of God, evil is not necessarily evil.

Although we recognize the meaning, and partial validity, of these and other arguments, they are not completely satisfying. How could they be? First, they are incredibly circular. Second, how do they help us to rid the world of evil—or in our terms, better *manage* the problem of evil?

To be perfectly frank, we don't know what to conclude. Unlike atheists, who take the presence of so much evil as strong evidence and proof that either God does not exist or, if God exists, he/she/it is not all loving, we do not necessarily reach such conclusions. The best we can do is admit that there are certain questions we can pose that are meaningful even if they are beyond our abilities to answer.

THE NATURE OF SPIRITUAL EXPERIENCE

If we are completely honest, we have to admit that logical arguments and philosophical reasoning take us only so far in apprehending the meaning of God, religion, and spirituality. This does not mean we should abandon logical arguments and philosophical reasoning all together, for to do so is a big step in the direction of fundamentalism—the unquestioned acceptance of our basic assumptions and beliefs.

Ideally, reason (cognitive IQ) and emotion (emotional IQ) should work together. The fact that they don't is one of the great sources of so many of our errors. If we are perfectly honest, we have to admit that writers, poets, and artists are often much better than scientists and philosophers at capturing the nature of religious and spiritual experiences:

For a moment, Isabel stood stock still. There were vegetables on the board before her, ready for the knife, but she did not move; her hand was arrested in its movement, motionless. She was aware of the physical sensation, sort of rushing within her and around her, a current, which seemed to fill her with warmth. She closed her eyes and, oddly, there was no darkness, just light. It was as if she were bathed in light both within and without.

. . . Later, with [her young baby] Charlie asleep, she and Jamie sat at the kitchen table. She had prepared scallops for them, to be followed by risotto, which she knew he liked. They had chilled white wine with the scallops, and he raised his glass to her, *to Charlie's mother.* She had laughed, and replied, *to his father.* She looked down at her plate. She wanted to tell him what had happened, there in the kitchen, while he was attending to Charlie, but how could she put it? *I had a mystical experience in the kitchen this evening?* Hardly. I'm not the sort who has mystical experiences in the kitchen, she said to herself; the world is divided between those who have mystical experiences in their kitchens and those who do not.[30]

THE JUST-IS PHILOSOPHY

The intelligibility of the universe itself needs explanation. It is therefore not the *gaps* in our understanding which point to God but rather the very *comprehensibility* of scientific and other forms of understanding that requires an explanation. In brief, the argument is that *explicability itself requires explanation. . . .* [31]

Atheists are fond of arguing that our universe *just is!* It doesn't require any superior or outside force to make it exist, for either it has always has existed, or the fact that our universe exists and has the properties it does is just a matter of probability, that is, raw statistics. If there are an infinite number of universes, then purely by chance one of them ought to exist wherein all the circumstances are just right for the emergence of life and intelligence as we know it. Purely by chance, all of the physical constants—for instance, gravity—ought to be lined up just right in one universe to allow galaxies and stars to form that ultimately result in intelligent life.

The cosmic flaw in the just-is philosophy is that in order for probability to operate, a more general mechanism is required. Presumably the infinite number of universes is ordered by a more general governing mechanism or principle so as to allow probability to operate in *all* universes. Invoking the notion of probability does not stop the need for an explanation; it only shifts it.

The kind of "sophisticated" atheist described earlier presumes to know not only that there is some (minimal) mechanism (probability) that generates an infinite number of universes, but also that every time a universe is created, its underlying constants are set (or reset) randomly. However, probability doesn't just drop from the skies, or universes. Probability is a distinct type of mechanism. As statisticians have learned, randomness is a very complex mechanism, especially pure randomness. A number of very severe and limiting conditions have to be satisfied in order for randomness to exist. In other words, there is a cosmic order underlying randomness.

Rather than knowing too little, the sophisticated atheist actually knows a great deal about not only our particular universe but also the entire set of universes. Minimal knowledge turns out to be maximal knowledge.

We do not doubt for one moment that the universe is governed by mechanisms and principles. God is the name for that mechanism and principle to the degree that the universe follows any mechanisms and principles at all.

CONCLUDING REMARKS

We close this chapter by commenting on its relationship to politics. The topic of religion and spirituality provides an interesting perspective on current affairs. When he was campaigning for the presidency, now President Barack Obama was roundly criticized, mostly by members of his own party, for embracing the concept of faith-based initiatives. The basic criticism was that in doing so he sounded too much like G. W. Bush "warmed over."

Democrats have extreme difficulty acknowledging not only the general role of emotions in life (the inner-individual and inner-group quadrants of Wilber's model) but also the role of religion and spirituality in particular. This has traditionally been one of the Democrats' greatest errors and downfalls. They just don't seem to understand—

to "get"—the powerful role that emotions and stories play in human affairs.[32] Indeed, stories play such a fundamental role that if we were inclined to believe that there are indeed "atoms" underlying all of human reality—which, given the arguments of the last chapter, we are not—then we would say that stories are it.

As this chapter has argued, not all forms of religion, and certainly not all forms of spirituality, are irrational. To the contrary, it is irrational *not* to believe in any form of religion and in spirituality.

We see little evidence that President Obama is in favor of "unreasoning" and "irrational" forms of faith. Nonetheless, unless Democrats learn very quickly the key role and extreme importance of religion and spirituality in personal and public life, they are doomed to fail.

Wags have often voiced the opinion that one of the worst things the Founding Fathers did was reject the idea of a state religion. If the United States had had a state religion, we might have ended up like Europe, that is, rejecting religion in large numbers. Perhaps then we would not have been as prone to fundamentalism, or in our terms, to solving the "wrong" problem of religion.

A GENERAL THEORY

OF ROTTENNESS

Breaking the Grip of Type Four Errors

A child . . . who had no important job and could only see things as his eyes
showed them to him, went up to the [Emperor's] carriage.

"The Emperor is naked," he said.

"Fool!" his father reprimanded, running after him. "Don't talk
nonsense!" He grabbed his child and took him away. But the boy's remark,
which had been heard by the bystanders, was repeated over and over again
until everyone cried:

"The boy is right! The Emperor is naked! It's true!"

The Emperor realized that the people were right but could not admit
to that. He thought it better to continue the procession under the illusion
that anyone who couldn't see his clothes was either stupid or incompetent.
And he stood stiffly on his carriage, while behind him a page held his
imaginary mantle.

—HANS CHRISTIAN ANDERSON, "The Emperor's New Clothes"[1]

If this Virginia Tech shooter had an ideology, what do you think it was?
This guy had to be a liberal?

—RUSH LIMBAUGH[2]

I was going to have a few comments on the other Democratic presidential,
John Edwards, but you have to go into rehab if you use the word faggot.[3]

—ANN COULTER

BY ANY STANDARD OF DECENCY

By almost any standard, these comments by Rush Limbaugh and Ann Coulter are extreme and nasty, if not outright sick and demented. One may be tempted, therefore, to dismiss them altogether as merely the crazy outbursts of a lunatic fringe. This is precisely what one must not do.

Unfortunately, Limbaugh's and Coulter's comments are representative of the sociopathic rumblings that all too often frequent the airwaves of present-day America. Ever since President Nixon learned that he could win by treading on the fears of voters, we've had forty years of hate talk. And it's only gotten worse.

Precisely because Limbaugh's and Coulter's comments are extreme and outrageous, not to mention illogical, they actually help us to see more clearly the motives and sentiments that underlie a great many Type Four Errors that are hidden under a veneer of acceptable speech. Furthermore, given Reverend Jeremiah Wright's inflammatory comments, foolishness and intemperate language span the political spectrum.

A GENERAL FRAMEWORK FOR UNDERSTANDING
AND TREATING TYPE FOUR ERRORS

This chapter presents a general framework for understanding how Errors of the Fourth Kind arise in the first place and what can be done to lessen their impacts, even if we cannot break free from them altogether. The chapter also discusses how "wicked problems" can be "partially tamed" and therefore managed somewhat. Taming wicked problems is the most important step for society to take, for it involves the management of Type Three and Type Four Errors.

Our general framework consists of three main parts:

1. The *underlying sources* of Errors of the Third and Fourth Kinds; these are the precipitating factors that motivate these errors.

2. The *means* by which Type Four errors are produced; these are the proximate causes of the errors.

3. The resulting effects, that is, the different *Errors* of the Third and Fourth Kinds themselves.

This general framework can be represented by a simple diagram:

Underlying Sources → Means → Type Four Errors.

The following lists present brief typologies of the various sources, means, and Errors that make up the framework. A word of caution is in order, however. The lists are neither exclusive nor exhaustive. They are not meant to be. The overlap between them is considerable because again we are dealing with a phenomenon that is inordinately complex and messy. For this reason, sources have an uncanny way of turning into means and Errors, and vice versa.

We begin with a list of the general sources, or underlying, precipitating causes, of Type Four Errors. They can be grouped according to four characteristic kinds of boundedness: (1) cognitive, (2) emotional and ethical, (3) institutional and social, and (4) spiritual and ethical.

Origins/Sources of the Type Three/Four Errors

I. *Cognitive boundedness:* possessing a narrow worldview and reducing all problems so that they fit into it. Persons who display this kind of boundedness often

1. cling to a narrow set of assumptions that may be the result of a limited education, a single all-encompassing ideology, or limited personal experiences, such as on the job.

2. believe that for every problem there is one and only one correct definition or formulation of the problem, and therefore that there is only one correct solution.

3. Believe that their own set of values is correct.

4. Display a low tolerance for ambiguity and complexity, that is, for "messes."

II. *Emotional and ethical roundedness:* a lack of empathy and respect for differing points of view. Persons who display this kind of boundedness often

1. display low tolerance for differing points of view and value systems, and feel the need to put down and discredit those that differ from theirs.

2. Deeply fear enemies—real and imagined.

3. Show a tendency to see defects, deficiencies, and problems in people or groups beyond their own circles, resulting in the demonization of others.

4. Idealize their own position.

III. *Institutional and social boundedness:* groupthink and the strong need for group approval. Persons who display this kind of boundedness often

1. maintain a tight reference group, organization, institution, profession, or discipline that reinforces and rewards conformity to its own narrow education, ideology, and set of values.

2. show a lack of faith and trust in public and private institutions outside their own reference group.

3. contribute to deep division within and across societies by ignoring the connectedness and interconnectedness among individuals and organizations and institutions.

IV. *Spiritual and ethical boundedness:* failure to appreciate and understand that there are higher stages of human development, and the corresponding failure to advance to those stages. Persons who display this kind of boundedness often

1. lack appreciation for overarching and shared belief systems and myths that give individuals and institutions meaning and purpose.

Next we offer a list of the means, or proximate causes, for most Type Four Errors. As with the sources, these can be grouped according to three principal categories:

I. Dirty tricks, lies, distortions, and assorted criminal acts

II. Projecting evil and the cause or source of all problems outward

III. Dumbing down and false simplicity

Means of Creating Type Four Errors

I. Dirty tricks, lies, distortions, and assorted criminal acts

1. Individual and institutional dirty tricks such as rigging elections and running dirty political campaigns, spreading lies, for example, swiftboating

2. Promoting guilt by association

3. Deliberate outright lying and fabricating the "big lie"

4. Repetition, that is, repeating the "big lie" over and over again

5. Not presenting the full or complete truth

6. Demonizing and ridiculing others

7. Orchestrated fear-mongering or paranoia

8. Constant blurring of the lines between truth and lies, news and entertainment, and so on

9. The orchestrated creation of sources of diversion

II. Projecting evil and the cause or source of all problems outward

1. Blaming others for one's problems

2. Creating enemies

3. Fomenting distrust

4. Orchestrating fear-mongering or paranoia

III. Dumbing down and false simplicity

1. Ignoring and downplaying complexity

2. Claiming that there are no other alternatives or choices than the ones presented

3. Reducing everything to a single measure, such as money

4. Using simple slogans and catchwords that make complex problems seem trivial

5. Emphasizing, exaggerating, or distorting the differences between experts

6. Emphasizing, exaggerating, or distorting the uncertainties in scientific research

Finally, following is a list of the general types of Type Four Errors that result from the various underlying sources and the means for producing them. The various types can be grouped into three categories:

I. Ethical and epistemic narrowness

II. Epistemic confusion

III. Confused and faulty argumentation

Different Forms/Types of the Type Three/Four Errors

I. Ethical and epistemic narrowness

1. Defining a problem too narrowly through the use of a single, preferred discipline, profession, ideology, worldview, set of values or assumptions, and so on; for example, partially formulating and solving a problem and thereby not solving the complete or full problem; drawing the boundaries of a problem too tightly and narrowly; and ignoring other and higher stages of human development and thereby contending that all problems can be formulated and solved at the stage one has reached

2. Ignoring other value systems, professions, ideologies, and worldviews; for example, contending that the benefits of a proposed solution outweigh the costs by defining both the benefits and the costs too narrowly or incompletely; reducing everything to a single variable, such as dollars

3. Discrediting other value systems, professions, ideologies, and worldviews; for example, ignoring that every problem has both technical and social dimensions

4. Focusing primarily, if not altogether, on certain stakeholders while ignoring and discrediting others

5. Ignoring complexity and messiness; faultily eliminating complexity and messiness through reductionism; for example, considering only "more leads to more" while ignoring the other paradoxes discussed in Chapter Four such as "more leads to less"

II. Epistemic Confusion

1. Confusing the difficulty in defining and solving complex, messy situations or problems by contending that they are impossible

2. Picking the wrong metrics, yardsticks, or methods and standards of evaluation

III. Confused and faulty argumentation: Unethical arguments

1. The deliberate or accidental use of faulty arguments to mislead the public

In Chapter Four we argued that the paradox "more leads to more," or "if at first you don't succeed, then just do more of the same," keeps us locked into committing the same Type Three and Type Four Errors over and over again. The trick, therefore, is not only how to break this pattern but how to break free from all of the forms and means of Type Three and Type Four Errors.

The short answer is: through the continued development and exercise of multiple intelligences—cognitive, emotional, ethical, and spiritual. Type Four Errors do not arise primarily through failure to think better and smarter. Rather, they arise through fear and narrowness. Traditional remedies of better education will not do the trick of breaking us free from their grip. Were we to formulate the problem of breaking the stranglehold of Type Four Errors primarily as a cognitive, an intellectual, and therefore an educational problem, we would thereby be guilty ourselves of committing a serious Error of the Fourth Kind. Errors of the Fourth Kind are simultaneously educational, economic, political, philosophical, and spiritual, and more. They must therefore be formulated as all of these or they cannot be formulated at all. We close this section with an example that is one of the most powerful illustrations of the need as well as the ability to think and act differently.

Although the anti-American Shiite cleric Moktada al-Sadr is clearly one of the worst of the insurgents against whom we are fighting in Iraq, he is also unfortunately one of the cleverest. Recently the *New York Times* reported that "[al-Sadr] has been working tirelessly to build support at the grass-roots level, opening storefront offices across Baghdad and southern Iraq that dispense services that are not being provided by the government. In this he seems to be following the model established by Hezbollah, the radical Lebanese Shiite group in Gaza, with entwined social and military wings that serve as a parallel government."[4] In short, al-Sadr has embraced a definition of the problem in Iraq that is rooted in the provision of social services.

In saying this, our intent is *not* to praise al-Sadr, and certainly *not* to praise Hezbollah, in the slightest. Both stand for things that we staunchly oppose. We cannot decouple al-Sadr's support of social services from his warlike tactics. Our focus on al-Sadr is only to show what *we* should be doing in Iraq, not to condone what he is doing or to praise him or his followers. We should be spending more time defining the terrible situation in Iraq as more than "a war to be won." Although it may be a war, it is also many, many more things, one of the most important being the extreme disruption of social services for those who need them most.

TAMING WICKED PROBLEMS

One of the most critical and thorniest issues we have to face is that of wicked problems. As introduced in Chapter Two, a wicked problem is a problem that resists formulation by any known discipline, profession, and so on. What, therefore, can we possibly do with them? As noted in Chapter Four, we can't just throw up our hands and do nothing, because doing nothing presupposes that the problem has been defined well enough that we can *know* that doing nothing is an acceptable option.

One idea is that we might take seriously (perhaps even literally) the notion that no discipline or profession has the solution and follow it through to its conclusion. The idea is Zen-like. We give up the thought of a completely disciplined way of approaching wicked problems, that is, we tame them by giving up the idea that we can *completely* tame them. This approach potentially opens up different ways of approaching such problems.

For example, we can look at a wicked problem from a totally different perspective. Suppose, for instance, that instead of looking at a such a problem as one of epistemology, of mustering the right kinds of knowledge to solve them, we were to look at them as matters of aesthetics, of how we view the world. This means we would have to turn to artists and poets to illuminate some of our most important issues. This is precisely what unconventional (aren't artists by definition?) artist Mark Lombardi accomplished.[5]

Long before 9/11, Lombardi developed intricate and elaborate ways of uncovering and tracing complex webs of international corruption. Part investigative reporter, postmodernist art historian, and graphic artist, Lombardi showed that by turning to public sources of information, he could demonstrate convincingly that bin Laden and the Bush family were connected through complex and nefarious financial dealings.

In short, Lombardi developed a new art form that showed pictorially how disparate and powerful global actors were interconnected. He showed the seamy side of the global economy and a "flat world" long before the term was even invented. As a result of his work, Lombardi was one of the few artists, if not the only one, to be accorded the dubious distinction of having his art examined by an FBI agent, in a museum no less, in order to gain clues into the terrorist financing of 9/11.

By citing the case of Lombardi we are of course not suggesting that wicked problems are the sole province of artists. We are suggesting nothing of the kind. What we are saying is that if wicked problems have any hope of being tamed (at least in part), it is only by the interplay of conventional and highly unconventional ways of looking at the world.

IDEOLOGY

Before we conclude, we need to say something about the role of ideology in wicked problems. One of the major dictionary definitions of ideology is "the ideas and manner of thinking characteristic of a group, social class, or individual."[6] The only word we would append to this definition is *narrow*, as in "the narrow ideas and manner of thinking characteristic of a group, social class, or individual." In our view, almost all ideologies are narrow and restricted. In this sense, ideology is one of the thorniest elements of all problems, big and small. What, then, are the prospects for "taming" ideology?

Once again, the diversity of thought on how to do so is instructive. One gets different "answers" depending on how one formulates the problem initially. For instance, according to Morley Winograd and Michael Hais, the problem of ideological rigidity is a "generational problem."[7] The Millennial Generation (roughly age twelve up to the early 30s) is proving to be remarkably free of the biases and prejudices of earlier generations. Race, gender, ethnic origins, and sexual orientation are comparably irrelevant to them.

The implication is clear: wait long enough and we will mature out of earlier biases and prejudices. Thus, for instance, unlike earlier generations, Millennials are not inherently opposed to universal health care provided by the federal government. This is in sharp contrast to the generation of the 1940s. Even though they would have benefited greatly from universal health care, poor Southern whites opposed it on the grounds that Southern hospitals would have to be integrated if the federal government provided it. Thus, they voted their racial interests over their health interests.

Another "answer," in terms of the ideas of Ken Wilber that we discussed in the last chapter, is that ideology is a function of where one is in the grand scheme of human development. And finally, the problem of ideology is viewed by some as just part of the ever-changing cycles of U.S. history.[8] According to Paul Krugman, recent winner of the Nobel Prize in Economics, the recent shift to a liberal or progressive ideology is due to the deep contradictions and imperfections inherent in conservative ideology.[9] For instance, the extreme close-mindedness of the Bush administration led it to appoint political cronies to sensitive positions, such as Michael Brown as the head of FEMA.

By now it should be obvious that we face a choice not between which theory is "right" and which are "wrong" but rather about what vital part each of them plays in understanding wicked problems. All of these perspectives are viable, and more. We need a 360-degree mirror in which to see ourselves clearly; we need multiple theories if we are to have any hope of explaining complex phenomena.

CONCLUDING REMARKS

Albert Einstein once said that a problem couldn't be solved in the same language in which it was originally expressed. We agree, but we also believe in something much stronger.

Problems cannot be *solved* at the level at which they are experienced because they cannot be correctly *formulated* at the level at which we experience them. Problems always require us to stand above them to better formulate them. Problems that are formulated at the particular stage of development of the person or society addressing them are invariably incomplete (see Chapter Eight). They embody all of the strengths and weakness (biases and pathologies) of a particular stage. In other words, people often remain stuck at whatever level of development they have attained. As a result, their definitions of key problems remain stuck as well.

Astute observer of American society Alexis De Tocqueville said it best of all: "It is easier for the world to accept a simple lie than a complex truth." The key, then, to breaking the grip of the errors that engulf us is to accept that there is no such thing as a problem that has a single solution, let alone a single formulation. For this reason, even though we have argued strongly for particular formulations of some of our most critical problems, such as health care, we are the first to realize that there is never—repeat, never—a single formulation of any important problem. Even if one accepts, as we do, that universal health care is a desirable and necessary goal, there are innumerable ways of achieving it.

Not only do our ideas about what it means to solve problems need to change drastically, but more fundamentally, our ideas regarding what it means to state problems in the first place need to change. If this is true, then in the end, the biggest problem facing us is how to formulate a better, that is, more comprehensive, theory of human and social development, and to learn how to apply it.

All of our lives we have been told "the Devil is in the details." This is only partially true at best. Long before we get to the details, the Devil is in the formulations we give to important problems. The Devil, after all, is very crafty. He wants us to put our enormous energies into solving the wrong problems. He wants us to get caught up in the details of the wrong problems.

NOTES

NOTES TO PREFACE

1. Marco Iacoboni, *Mirroring People: The New Science of How We Connect with Others* (New York: Farrar, Straus, and Giroux, 2008).

2. Jerome Groopman, *How Doctors Think* (New York: Houghton Mifflin, 2007).

3. One of the few exceptions is an earlier book by the first author: Ian I. Mitroff, *Smart Thinking for Crazy Times: The Art of Solving the Right Problems* (San Francisco: Berrett-Koehler, 1999). However, even this book does not go far enough in identifying and treating the general phenomenon.

4. The closest are the innumerable books on creativity and problem solving. However, virtually none of these treat explicitly the error of solving the wrong problems precisely.

NOTES TO CHAPTER I

1. Quoted in Gary Oehlert, "Asking Good Questions," online PowerPoint slides, School of Statistics, University of Minnesota, March 31, 2008; for a biography of Tukey, see David R. Brillinger, "John W. Tukey: His Life and Professional Contributions," *The Annals of Statistics* 30, no. 6 (2002): 1535–1575.

2. Howard Raiffa, *Decision Analysis: Introductory Lectures on Choices Under Uncertainty* (Reading, PA: Addison-Wesley, 1968); for an alternate discussion of the Type Three Error, see A. W. Kimball, "Errors of the Third Kind in Statistical Consulting," *Journal of the American Statistical Association* 52, no. 278 (June 1957): 133–142.

3. In more technical terms, when we commit a Type One Error, we reject the hypothesis that the old drug is as good as (equal to) or better than the new drug when the old drug is actually better. That is, we should have instead accepted the hypothesis that the old drug is as good as (equal to) or better than the new drug. Conversely, we commit a Type Two Error when we reject the hypothesis that the new drug is as good as (equal to) or better than the old drug when the new drug is actually better.

4. The details of the Belgium Coca-Cola crisis were derived from various Web sites found by Googling the Coca-Cola Belgium crisis. See also note 9.

5. Readers who are familiar with attachment theory will immediately recognize the term *avoidant*. To those readers who are not familiar with it, we recommend the excellent overview by Robert Karen, *Becoming Attached: Unfolding the Mystery of the Infant-Mother Bond and Its Impact on Later Life* (New York: Warner Books, 1994).

6. At an early age, avoidants essentially gave up all hope of getting their basic emotional needs met by their primary caregivers. Ignoring others is really a defense against acknowledging the deep disappointments and hurt they experienced when they were very young.

7. Ibid.

8. Ibid.

9. ICMR Center for Management Research, "Coca-Cola's Belgian Crisis—The Public Relations Fiasco," http://www.icmrindia.org/casestudies/catalogue/Marketing/Coca-Cola%20Belgian%20Crisis-Public%20Relations%20Fiasco-Marketing%20Case%20Study.htm

10. Groopman, *How Doctors Think*.

11. Robert Reich, *Supercapitalism: The Transformation of Business, Democracy, and Everyday Life* (New York: Knopf, 2007); Naomi Klein, *The Shock Doctrine: The Rise of Disaster Capitalism* (New York: Metropolitan Books, 2007).

12. Joel Bakan, *The Corporation* (New York: Free Press 2004).

13. Karen Armstrong, *The Great Transformation: The Beginning of Our Religious Traditions* (New York: Anchor Books, 2007); the reader is especially referred to Charles Taylor's masterful account, *A Secular Age* (Cambridge, MA: Harvard University Press, 2007).

14. Ian I. Mitroff, *The Subjective Side of Science: A Philosophical*

Inquiry into the Psychology of the Apollo Moon Scientists (Amsterdam: Elsevier, 1974; reissued Seaside, CA: Intersystems, 1984).

15. Ibid.

16. Jeffrey Goldberg, "Party Unfaithful," *New Yorker*, June 4, 2007, 42; italics added.

17. George Lakoff, *The Political Mind: Why You Can't Understand 21st-Century American Politics with an 18th-Century Brain* (New York: Viking, 2008).

18. Thomas Wagner, AP Wire, http://news.yahoo.com (accessed July 3, 2007).

19. Nancy Gibbs, "Darkness Falls," *TIME*, April 30, 2007, 48; italics added.

NOTES TO CHAPTER 2

1. Russell L. Ackoff, *Re-Creating the Corporation* (New York: Oxford University Press, 1999), 324; italics in original.

2. Ackoff, *Re-Creating the Corporation*, 178–179; italics added.

3. Russell L. Ackoff, *The Democratic Corporation* (New York: Oxford University Press, 1994).

4. Horst Rittel and Melvin Webber, "Dilemmas in a General Theory of Planning," *Policy Sciences* 4 (1973): 155–169.

5. As with most things academic, there is a long and extensive literature on ill-structured problems. There is also considerable debate as to who coined the term *ill-structured problem* and when: Russell L. Ackoff, *Redesigning the Future: A Systems Approach to Societal Programs* (New York: Wiley, 1974); C. West Churchman, *The Design of Inquiring Systems: Basic Concepts of Systems and Organization* (New York: Basic Books, 1971); J. Dewey, *How We Think: A Restatement of the Relation of Reflective Thinking to the Educative Process* (Boston: Heath, 1933); K. A. Harper, "Expert-Novice Comparisons to Illuminate Differences in Perceptions of Problem Solutions," *AIP Conference Proceedings*, no. 720 (2004): 129–132; H. A. Hembrooke, G. K. Gay, and L. A. Granka, "The Effects of Expertise and Feedback on Search Term Selection and Subsequent Learning," *Journal of the American Society for Information Science and Technology* 56, no. 8 (2005): 861–871; D. H. Jonassen, "Instructional Design Models for Well-Structured and Ill-Structured Problem-Solving Learning Outcomes," *Educational Technology Research and Development* 45, no. 1 (1997): 65–94;

D. H. Jonassen, "Toward a Design Theory of Problem Solving," *Educational Technology Research and Development* 48, no. 4 (2000): 63–85; S. P. Lajoie, "Transitions and Trajectories for Studies of Expertise," *Educational Researcher* 32, no. 8 (2003): 21–25; A. Newell and H. A. Simon, *Human Problem Solving* (Englewood Cliffs, NJ: Prentice-Hall, 1972); A. Newell and H. A. Simon, "Computer Science as Empirical Inquiry: Symbols and Search," *Communications of the ACM* 19, no. 3 (1976): 113–126; M. Polanyi, *The Tacit Dimension* (Garden City, NY: Anchor Books, 1967); M. Prince and B. Hoyt, "Helping Students Make the Transition from Novice to Expert Problem-Solvers," 32nd ASEE/IEEE Frontiers in Education Conference, Boston, MA, November 6–9, 2002, Vol. 2 (2002): F2A-7-11; H. A. Simon, "Structure of Ill-Structured Problems," *Artificial Intelligence* 4, no. 3–4 (1973): 181–201; J. D. Sinnott, "A Model for Solution of Ill-Structured Problems: Implications for Everyday and Abstract Problem Solving," in J. D. Sinnott, ed., *Everyday Problem Solving: Theory and Applications* (New York: Praeger, 1989), 73–99; J. F. Voss and T. A. Post, "On the Solving of Ill-Structured Problems," in M.T.H. Chi, R. Glaser, and M. J. Farr, eds., *The Nature of Expertise* (Hillsdale, NJ: Lawrence Erlbaum, 1988), 261–285; A. Wetzstein and W. Hacker, "Reflective Verbalization Improves Solutions: The Effects of Question-Based Reflection in Design Problem Solving," *Applied Cognitive Psychology* 18, no. 2 (2004): 145–156; S. S. Wineburg, "Historical Problem Solving: A Study of the Cognitive Processes Used in the Evaluation of Documentary and Pictorial Evidence," *Journal of Educational Psychology* 83, no. 1 (1991): 73–87; G. E. Xun and S. M. Land, "A Conceptual Framework for Scaffolding Ill-Structured Problem-Solving Processes Using Question Prompts and Peer Interactions," *Educational Technology Research and Development* 52, no. 2 (2004): 5–22.

6. Ackoff, *Re-Creating the Corporation.*

7. George Lakoff, *Moral Politics* (Chicago: University of Chicago Press, 1996); we have also benefitted from discussions with Drexel Sprecher; Ken Wilber, *A Brief History of Everything* (Boston: Shambhala, 1996).

8. Bill Bishop, *The Big Sort: Why the Clustering of Like-Minded America Is Tearing Us Apart* (New York: Houghton Mifflin, 2008); George Lakoff, *The Political Mind: Why You Can't Understand 21st-Century American Politics with an 18th-Century Brain* (New York: Viking, 2008).

9. Lakoff, *Moral Politics.*

10. "How to Live Forever," *Economist*, January 5, 2008, 76–77.

NOTES TO CHAPTER 3

1. D. V. Cutler, *Your Money or Your Life: Strong Medicine for America's Healthcare System* (New York: Oxford University Press, 2004), 100.

2. Cutler, *Your Money*, 122–123; italics added.

3. Helen Dewar, "Biden, Home on the Hill," *Washington Post*, September 8, 1988, C1; Rene Hertlinger, *Market-Driven Health Care* (New York: Basic Books, 1997), 99.

4. Kevin Lamb, "How Well Does 'Sick' Stick to the Facts?" *New York Times News Service*, July 5, 2007.

5. The Commonwealth Fund Commission on a Higher Performance Health System. "Why Not the Best? Results from a National Scorecard on U.S. Health System Performance." September 20, 2006. Available at http://www.commonwealthfund.org/Content/Publications/Fund-Reports/2006/Sep/Why-Not-the-Best—Results-from-a-National-Scorecard-on-U-S—Health-System-Performance.aspx

6. Ezekiel J. Emanuel, "What Cannot Be Said on Television About Health Care," *JAMA: Journal of the American Medical Association* 297, no. 19 (2007), 2131–2133.

7. Ibid.

8. Michael E. Porter and Elizabeth Olmsted Teisberg, *Redefining Health Care: Creating Value-Based Competition on Results* (Boston: Harvard Business School Press, 2006), 47.

9. Cutler, *Your Money*.

10. Crystal Phend, "Pneumonia Vaccine Slashed Health Care Costs in Children," *Med Page Today*, December 4, 2007.

11. Porter and Teisberg, *Redefining Health Care.*

12. John Carryrou, "As Medical Costs Soar the Insured Faces Freeze Tab," *Wall Street Journal*, November 29, 2007.

13. Centers for Disease Control and Prevention, "Chronic Disease Overview," accessed November 18, 2005, at http://www.cdc.gov/NCCd php/overview.htm; Spyros Andreopoulos, "How To End the Health Care Reform Deadlock," *San Francisco Chronicle*, October 10, 2007.

14. *Health Affairs*, press release, October 20, 2004; available at http://www.healthaffairs.org/press/septoct0405.htm.

15. Marcia Angell, *The Truth About the Drug Companies: How They Deceive Us and What to Do About It* (New York: Random House, 2005);

J. Paul Leigh and James Fries, "Health Habits, Health Care Use, and Costs in a Sample of Retirees," *Inquiry* 29 (Spring 1992), 44–54.

16. Arnold S. Relman, M.D., "Medical Professionalism in a Commercialized Health Care Market," *JAMA: The Journal of the American Medical Association* 298, no. 22 (December 12, 2007), 2668–2670.

17. Kenneth J. Arrow, "Uncertainty and the Welfare Economics of Medical Care," *American Economic Review* 53, no. 5 (1963), 941–973.

18. Victoria Colliver, "Insurance Is at a Premium, People Between 50 and 64 Have a Tough Time Getting Health Coverage," *San Francisco Chronicle*, 2007, p. C-2.

19. Victoria Colliver, "Lawsuit Claims Health Net Gave Bonuses for Policy Rescissions," San Francisco Chronicle, November 10, 2007. Available at http://www.sfgate.com/cgi-bin/article.cgi?f=/c/a/2007/11/10/ BUCLT9JOV.DTL

20. Hector De La Torre and A. S. Mohal, "And They Thought They Had Insurance," *San Francisco Chronicle*, October 12, 2007, p. B-11.

21. Ricardo Alonzo-Zaldevar, "The Catch in GOP Contenders' Health Plans," *San Francisco Chronicle*, November 21, 2007, p. A-6.

22. Amy Lorentzen, "McCain Wants Health Care Overhaul, with Tax Credits," *Associated Press*, October 2, 2007.

23. Angell, *The Truth*.

24. Betty Hileman, "Regulatory Trends," *Chemical and Engineering News* 84, no. 25 (June 19, 2006): 80–99.

25. Ibid.

26. Hileman, "Regulatory Trends."

27. Salomeh Keyhani, Marie Diener-West, and Neil Powe, "Are Development Times for Pharmaceuticals Increasing or Decreasing?" *Health Affairs* 25, no. 2 (2006): 461–468.

28. Hileman,"Regulatory Trends."

29. Ibid.

30. Peggy Peck, "Genentech eases stance on Bevacizumb (Avastin) for macular degeneration." Accessed November 1, 2007 at http://www.med pagetoday.com

31. M. Kutner, E. Greenberg, Y. Jin, and C. Paulsen, "The Health Literacy of America's Adults: Results from the 2003 National Assessment of Adult Literacy (NAAL)," NCES2006-483 (Washington, DC: National Center for Education Statistics, U.S. Department of Education, 2006).

32. Kutner, Greenberg, Jin, and Paulsen, "The Health Literacy of America's Adults."

33. G. M. Lawrie, G. C. Morris Jr., J. H. Calhoon, H. Safi, J. L. Samora, M. Beltangady, A. Baron, A. Silvers, and D. W. Chapman, "Clinical Results of Coronary Bypass in 500 Patients at Least Ten Years After Operation," *Circulation* Supplement I: I-1 through I-5 (1982).

34. Robert Kuttner, *The Squandering of America* (New York: Knopf, 2007), 32.

35. Angell, *The Truth*.

36. Ibid.

NOTES TO CHAPTER 4

1. Russell Ackoff, *Creating the Corporate Future* (New York: Wiley, 1981), 34–35.

2. Joseph E. Stiglitz and Linda Bilmes, *The Three Trillion Dollar War: The True Cost of the Iraq Conflict* (New York: Norton, 2008).

3. Ian I. Mitroff, "The Complete and Utter Failure of Traditional Thinking in Comprehending the Nuclear Predicament: Why It's Impossible to Formulate a Paradox Free Theory of Nuclear Policy," *Technological Forecasting and Social Change* 29 (1986): 51–72; reprinted in *A Science of Goal Formulation: American and Soviet Discussions of Cybernetics and Systems Theory*, ed. Stuart A. Umpleby and Vadin Sadovsky (New York: Hemisphere, 1991), 19–48.

4. For a complimentary analysis, see Jonathon Schell, *The Seventh Decade: The New Shape of Nuclear Danger* (New York: Henry Holt, 2007).

5. Gregory F. Treverton, "Risks and Riddles: The Soviet Union Was a Puzzle. Al Qaeda Is a Mystery. Why We Need to Know the Difference," *Smithsonian Magazine* (June 2007); available at http://www.smithsonian mag.com/people-places/presence_puzzle.html; first-paragraph italics in original, second- and third-paragraph italics added.

6. The authors thank an anonymous reviewer for making this point.

7. Charles Perrow, *Organizing America: Wealth, Power, and the Origins of American Capitalism* (Princeton, NJ: Princeton University Press, 2002), 217–218; italics added.

8. Ibid., 224–225; italics added.

9. "Nuclear Weapons in a New World," *Scientific American* (October 14, 2007): 74.

10. Jonathon Schell, "The Old and New Shapes of Nuclear Danger," *The Nation* (December 24, 2007): 17.

11. More accurately, an army battalion has between 400 and 1,000 people, while an army company has from 100 to 250 people.

12. Ackoff, *Creating the Corporate Future*.

NOTES TO CHAPTER 5

1. "Notebook," *TIME*, December 6, 2004; italics added.

2. For instance, see Arthur Schlesinger Jr., *The Cycles of American History* (New York: Mariner Books, 1999).

3. Frank Rich, *The Greatest Story Ever Sold: The Decline and Fall of Truth in Bush's America* (New York: Penguin, 2007). See also Michael Isikoff and David Korn, *Hubris: The Inside Story of Spin, Scandal, and the Selling of the Iraq War* (New York: Three Rivers Press, 2007); Eugen Seunda and Terrenc Moran, *Selling War to America: From the Spanish American War to the Global War on Terror* (Westport, CT: Praeger Security International, 2007); Jon Western, *Selling Intervention and War: The Presidency, the Media, and the American Public* (Baltimore, MD: Johns Hopkins University Press, 2005).

4. James Frey, *A Million Little Pieces* (New York: Anchor-Doubleday, 2006).

5. Thomas L. Friedman, *The World Is Flat: A Brief History of the Twenty-First Century* (New York: Farrar, Straus, and Giroux, 2005).

6. See http://www.americandialect.org/index.php/amerdial/2006/01

7. Frank Rich, "Truthiness 101: From Frey to Alito," *New York Times*, January 22, 2006; available at http://select.nytimes.com/2006/01/22/opinion/22rich.html?_r=1

8. Russell Ackoff, *The Democratic Corporation* (New York: Oxford University Press, 1994.); see also Russell Ackoff and Fred Emery, *On Purposeful Systems* (Chicago: Aldine-Atherton, 1972).

9. Katharine Washburn and John Thornton, eds., *Dumbing Down: Essays on the Strip-Mining of American Culture* (New York: Norton, 1996).

10. For two important analyses of this phenomenon, see Robert Reich, *Tales of a New America* (New York: Times Books, 1987); and Rupert Wilkerson, *The Pursuit of American Character* (New York: Harper and Row,

1988). See also William Strauss and Neil Howe, *The Fourth Turning: An American Prophecy* (New York: Broadway Books, 1997).

11. See Jean Baudrillard, *Selected Writings,* ed. Mark Poster (Stanford, CA: Stanford University Press, 1988).

12. The literature dealing with the various aspects of unreality is by now so vast that we can give only a sampling: Sam Brenton and Reuben Cohen, *Shooting People: Adventures in Reality TV* (New York: Verso, 2003); Charles Crittenden, *Unreality: The Metaphysics of Fictional Objects* (Ithaca, NY: Cornell University Press, 1991); William Damon, *Greater Expectations: Overcoming the Culture of Indulgence in Our Homes and Schools* (New York: Free Press, 1995); John de Graaf, David Wann, and Thomas H. Naylor, *Affluenza: The All-Consuming Epidemic* (San Francisco: Berrett-Koehler, 2001); James Friedman, ed., *Reality Squared: Televisual Discourse on the Real* (New Brunswick, NJ: Rutgers University Press, 2002); Frank Furedi, *Where Have All the Intellectuals Gone? Confronting 21st-Century Philistinism* (New York: Continuum, 2004); Joel Garreau, *Radical Evolution: The Promise and Peril of Enhancing Our Minds, Our Bodies—and What It Means to Be Human* (New York: Doubleday, 2004); Kevin Glynn, *Tabloid Culture: Trash, Taste, Popular Power, and the Transformation of American Television* (Durham, NC: Duke University Press, 2000); Jeffrey Goldstein, David Buckingham, and Gilles Brougere, eds., *Toys, Games, and Media* (Mahwah, NJ: Erlbaum, 2004); Susan A. Greenfield, *The Private Life of the Brain* (New York: Wiley, 2000); N. Katherine Hayles, *How We Became Posthuman: Virtual Bodies in Cybernetics, Literature, and Infomatics* (Chicago: University of Chicago Press, 1999); Mark Hertsgaard, *The Eagle's Shadow: Why America Fascinates and Infuriates the World* (London: Bloomsbury, 2002); Richard Hofstadter, *Anti-Intellectualism in American Life* (New York: Vintage Books, 1962); Su Colmes and Deborah Jermyn, eds., *Understanding Reality Television* (New York: Routledge, 2004); Jacques Houis, Paola Mieli, and Mark Stafford, eds., *Being Human: The Technological Extensions of the Body* (New York: Agincourt/Marsilio, 1999); Russell Jacoby, *The Last Intellectuals: American Culture in the Age of Academe* (New York: Basic Books, 1987); Ray Kurzweil, *The Age of Spiritual Machines: When Computers Exceed Human Intelligence* (New York: Penguin Books, 1999); Janet H. Murray, *Hamlet on the Holodeck: The Future of Narrative in Cyberspace* (Cambridge, MA: MIT Press, 1997); Susan Murray and Laurie Ouellette, eds., *Reality TV: Remaking*

Television Culture (New York: New York University Press, 2004); Robert B. Reich, *Tales of a New America* (New York: Times Books, 1987); Tom Reichert and Jacqueline Lambiase, *Sex in Advertising: Perspectives on the Erotic Appeal* (Mahwah, NJ: Erlbaum, 2003); Ziauddin Sadar and Merryl Wyn Davies, *Why Do People Hate America?* (Cambridge, UK: Icon Books, 2004); Ziauddin Sadar and Merryl Wyn Davies, *American Dream: Global Nightmare* (Cambridge, UK: Icon Books, 2004); Juliet Schor, *Born to Buy: The Commercialized Child and the New Consumer Culture* (New York: Scribner, 2004); Mark Slouka, *War of the Worlds: Cyberspace and the High-Tech Assault on Reality* (New York: Basic Books, 1995); Matthew Smith and Andrew Wood, eds., *Survivor Lessons: Essays on Communication and Reality Television* (Jefferson, NC: McFarland, 2003); Steve Stark, *Glued to the Set: The 60 Television Shows and Events that Made Us Who We Are Today* (New York: Free Press, 1997); Gerald Swanson, *America the Broke: How the Reckless Spending of the White House and Congress Are Bankrupting Our Country and Destroying Our Children's Future* (New York: Currency-Doubleday, 2004); Leo Sweeney, William J. Carroll, and John J. Furlong, *Authentic Metaphysics in an Age of Unreality* (San Francisco: Peter Lang, 1993); James W. Walters, *What Is a Person?* (Urbana: University of Illinois Press, 1997); Noah Wardrip-Fruin and Pat Harrigan, eds., *First Person: News Media as Story, Performance and Game* (Cambridge, MA: MIT Press, 2004); Washburn and Thorton, *Dumbing Down;* Robert J. Weber, *The Created Self: Reinventing Body, Persona, and Spirit* (New York: Norton, 2000); Gabriel Weimann, *Communicating Unreality: Modern Media and the Reconstruction of Reality* (Thousand Oaks, CA: Sage, 2000); Don Welton, ed., *The Body* (Malden, MA: Blackwell, 1999); Thomas H. Wheeler, *Photo Truth or Photo Fiction? Ethics in Media, Imagery in the Digital Age* (Mahwah, NJ: Erlbaum, 2002); Rupert Wilkinson, *The Pursuit of American Character* (New York: Harper & Row, 1988); Alan Wolfe, *One Nation, After All: What Middle-Class Americans Really Think About* (New York: Penguin Books, 1998); Alan Wolfe, *Return to Greatness: How America Lost Its Sense of Purpose and What It Needs to Do to Recover It* (Princeton, NJ: Princeton University Press, 2005); Dolf Zillman and Peter Vorderer, eds., *Media Entertainment: The Psychology of Its Appeal* (Mahwah, NJ: Erlbaum, 2000).

13. Julian Dibbell, "A Rape in Cyberspace: How an Evil Clown, a Haitian Trickster Spirit, Two Wizards, and a Cast of Dozens Turned a

Database Into a Society," *Village Voice*, December 23, 1993; available at
http://www.juliandibbell.com/texts/bungle_vv.html

14. *Reuter's*, December 18, 2004.

15. Kevin Warwick, "Cyborg 1.0" *Wired* (February 2000): 151.

16. Guy Womack, attorney for Charles Graner, in opening arguments
to the U.S. military jury at the reservist's court martial on charges of abus-
ing Iraqi prisoners at Abu Ghraib prison.

17. "Co. to Advertise on Neb. Man's Forehead," Associated Press,
January 25, 2005.

18. George Lakoff, *Moral Politics* (Chicago: University of Chicago
Press, 1996).

19. Terry Southern, *The Magic Christian* (New York: Grove Press,
1959), 22–27.

20. Lynn Smith, "Fox 'Daddy' Draws Ire," *Los Angeles Times* (December 22, 2004), E1.

NOTES TO CHAPTER 6

1. Ian I. Mitroff, "A Study of Computer-Aided Engineering Design"
(PhD diss., University of California, Berkeley, 1967).

2. The difference between force and stress is as follows: Stress is force
divided by area. If we have two five-pound bricks, then the force they exert
on a table that has to support them is the same—their weight, or five pounds.
However, if the area of one brick is five square inches and the other is fifty
square inches, then the first brick places a pressure of five pounds divided
by five square inches or one pound per square inch on the table. However,
the second brick only places a pressure of five pounds divided by fifty square
inches or one-tenth of a pound per square inch. The brick with the larger
area distributes its weight over a larger surface and thus reduces the pressure on the table. The same applies to the walls or thickness of a pressure
vessel. A pressure vessel with thicker walls has a greater area in which to
bear an equal force than a pressure vessel with thinner walls. Thus, the
pressure vessel with thicker walls has a lower stress for the same amount
of force than a pressure vessel with thinner walls.

3. In addition, Bill could fiddle with another important variable known
as the *safety factor*. Because all of the equations of science and engineering
are based on ideal models, phenomena in the real world do not always fit
into them perfectly. As a result, the theoretical calculations of the necessary

thickness of a pressure vessel, for instance, are multiplied by an appropriate safety factor to improve the margin of safety of a real design. Typically, safety factors are in the range of 1.10 to 1.25. That is, the theoretical thickness is increased by approximately 10 to 25 percent. The point is that Bill had room to maneuver in selecting a safety factor.

4. Rakesh Khurana, *From Higher Aims to Hired Hands: The Social Transformation of American Business Schools and the Unfulfilled Promise of Management as a Profession* (Princeton, NJ: Princeton University Press, 2007).

5. Cara Buckley, "Why Our Hero Leapt from the Tracks and Why We Might Not," *New York Times* (January 7, 2007): 3.

6. Cara Buckley, "Patience, Fairness, and the Human Condition," *The Economist* (October 6, 2007): 93; italics in original.

7. For purposes of confidentiality, the student's name and the dissertation topic have been omitted.

8. Thomas L. Friedman, *The World Is Flat: A Brief History of the Twenty-First Century* (New York: Farrar, Straus, and Giroux, 2005).

9. Mary Midgley, *The Myths We Live By* (Oxford, UK: Routledge, 2003), 27.

NOTES TO CHAPTER 7

1. Jeffrey Kluger, "Why We Worry About the Things We Shouldn't . . . and Ignore the Things We Should," *TIME*, December 4, 2006, 71.

2. Ian I. Mitroff, *The Subjective Side of Science: A Philosophical Inquiry into the Psychology of the Apollo Moon Scientists* (Amsterdam: Elsevier, 1974; reissued Seaside, CA: Intersystems, 1984).

3. S. James Press and Judith Turner, *The Subjectivity of Scientists and the Bayesian Approach* (New York: Wiley Interscience, 2001).

4. Michael J. Mahoney, "Publication Prejudices: An Experimental Study of Confirmatory Bias in the Peer Review System," *Cognitive Therapy and Research* 1, no. 2 (1977): 161–175.

5. There are of course many more than just five ways of producing knowledge, that is, many more than just five systems of inquiry. To contend otherwise would be absurd. Indeed, what form of inquiry would we have to use to determine that there are five and only five such systems? The five that are covered in this chapter are merely a good starting point. For a more in-depth treatment of these five systems, see C. West Churchman,

The Design of Inquiring Systems (New York: Basic Books, 1971); E. A. Singer Jr., *Experience and Reflection* (Philadelphia: University of Pennsylvania Press, 1959); Ian I. Mitroff and Harold A. Linstone, *The Unbounded Mind: Breaking the Chains of Traditional Thinking* (New York: Oxford University Press, 1993).

6. This example is taken from papers written by several students in Mitroff's classes.

7. An inquiry system consists of *inputs* and an *operator* who transforms the inputs into *outputs,* which are then regarded as the "truth." One of the most critical features of an inquiry system is what Churchman (*The Design of Inquiring Systems*) labels the *guarantor:* that which "guarantees" that if one starts with the "right kind of inputs" and operates on them in the "right way," the outputs of the system will be the "truth." In the expert consensus model, the tighter—that is, stronger—the agreement is between the experts, the more closely it will approach the truth. Thus, the guarantor is the agreement between independent experts. Notice that the guarantor and the operator are intertwined. That is, they are not independent. Agreement is both the operator—it is used to manufacture the output—and the guarantor of the system. For this reason, it is well-advised to be suspicious of how agreement is obtained, such as whether or not it is forced.

8. Thomas L. Friedman, *The World Is Flat: A Brief History of the Twenty-First Century* (New York: Farrar, Straus, and Giroux, 2005).

9. Michael Kinsley, "In Defense of Partisan Bickering," *TIME* (February 5, 2007): 41; italics added.

10. Once we have all of the various methods at our disposal, we can use them in various combinations. The important point is that the pure methods, systems, or models, let alone their combinations, are rarely discussed in the arena of business.

11. See the previous note.

12. Quoted in David Marcum and Steven Smith, *Egonomics* (New York: Simon and Schuster, 2007), 132.

13. Lesley A. Sharp, *Strange Harvest* (Berkeley: University of California Press, 2006).

14. Ibid.

15. See Churchman, *Design of Inquiring Systems;* and Singer, *Experience and Reflection.*

16. Churchman, *Design of Inquiring Systems.*

17. Mitroff, *The Subjective Side*.

18. Marco Iacoboni, *Mirroring People: The New Science of How We Connect with Others* (New York: Farrar, Straus, and Giroux, 2008).

19. Ibid.

20. Ambrose Bierce, *The Devil's Dictionary* (New York: Doubleday, 1906).

21. Thomas L. Friedman, *The World Is Flat: A Brief History of the Twenty-First Century* (New York: Farrar, Straus, and Giroux, 2005).

22. John Dewey, *The Quest for Certainty* (New York: Putnam, 1960).

23. E. J. Dionne Jr., "The Meaning of Bipartisanship Talk—Nothing," *San Francisco Chronicle* (January 9, 2007): B7.

24. See Henry Mintzberg, *Managers, Not MBAs* (San Francisco: Berrett-Koehler, 2004) for a fascinating and critical history of business schools.

25. Thomas L. Friedman, *The World Is Flat*.

NOTES TO CHAPTER 8

1. Karen Armstrong, *The Great Transformation: The Beginning of Our Religious Traditions* (New York: Anchor Books, 2007), 166; first italics added, second italics in original.

2. See Sam Harris, *The End of Faith* (New York: Norton, 2004); Richard Dawkins, *The God Delusion* (New York: Houghton Mifflin, 2006); Christopher Hitchens, *God Is Not Great: How Religion Poisons Everything* (New York: Twelve, 2007); Chris Hedges, *I Don't Believe in Atheists* (New York: Free Press, 2008). For an even harsher criticism of Harris and others, see Alister McGrath and Joanna Collicutt McGrath, *The Dawkins Delusion* (Downers Grove, IL: IVP Books, 2007), 31.

3. Armstrong, *The Great Transformation;* the reader is especially referred to Charles Taylor's excellent account, *A Secular Age* (Cambridge, MA: Harvard University Press, 2007).

4. For a masterful discussion of this point, see Mary Midgley, *The Myths We Live By* (New York: Routledge, 2004).

5. Ibid.

6. For an excellent introduction to the history of God and religion, see Mark Lilla, *The Stillborn God: Religion, Politics, and the Modern West* (New York: Knopf, 2007).

7. Thomas Hobbes, *Leviathan* (New York: Penguin, New York, 1982).

8. Ken Wilber is so prolific a writer that we can cite here only a few of his many works (all but the last published by Shambhala in Boston): *A Brief History of Everything* (1996); *No Boundary* (2001); *Integral Psychology* (2000); *Sex, Ecology, and Spirituality* (1995); *A Theory of Everything* (2000); for the most comprehensive treatment of Wilber's theory of spirituality, see *Integral Spirituality* (Boston: Integral Books, 2006).

9. See Armstrong, *The Great Transformation*.

10. For a sharp critique of hierarchy, and of Ken Wilber's work in particular, see Jorge N. Ferrer, *Revisioning Transpersonal Psychology: A Participatory Vision of Human Spirituality* (Albany: State University of New York Press, 2002).

11. See previously listed works by Wilber.

12. What follows is of course our interpretation of Wilber. It is not necessarily Wilber's own point of view.

13. Edward Hall, *The Silent Language* (New York: Anchor Books, 1973).

14. Spirituality is in fact what gave rise to Wilber's framework in the first place.

15. See Wilber's previously listed works.

16. See Midgley, *The Myths We Live By*.

17. Clare Graves, "Summary Statement: The Emergent, Cyclical, Double-Helix Model of the Adult Human Biopsychosocial Systems," Boston, May 20, 1981; Don Beck and Christopher Cowan, *Spiral Dynamics* (Boston: Blackwell, 1996).

18. Once again, we are not saying that there are literally nine and only nine stages. Rather, the notion of stages must be taken with a grain of salt, that is, as a heuristic device that allows us to make sense of an inordinately complex phenomenon. For a penetrating discussion of stages in Western civilization, see Charles Taylor, *A Secular Age*. For a particular discussion of the evolution of the idea of equality, see Lynn Hunt, *Inventing Human Rights: A History* (New York: Norton, 2007).

19. See *Mythology Pictures* (Amsterdam: Pepin Press, 2006).

20. Cynthia Stokes Brown, *Big History: From the Big Bang to the Present* (New York: New Press, 2007).

21. Ibid.

22. Ibid.

23. Thomas L. Friedman, *The World Is Flat: A Brief History of the Twenty-First Century* (New York: Farrar, Straus, and Giroux, 2005).

24. See Sallie McFague, *Models of God: Theology for an Ecological, Nuclear Age* (Philadelphia: Fortress Press, 1987).

25. See Brian Davies and G. R. Evans, eds., *Anselm of Canterbury: The Major Works* (Oxford, UK: Oxford University Press, 1998).

26. See William Lane Craig, *The Cosmological Argument from Plato to Leibniz* (Eugene, OR: Wipf and Stock, 2001); J. L. Mackie, *The Miracle of Theism: Arguments For and Against the Existence of God* (Oxford, UK: Clarendon Press, 1982); Alvin Plantinga and Nicholas Wolterstorff, eds., *Faith and Rationality: Reason and Belief in God* (Notre Dame, IN: University of Notre Dame Press, 1983); Alvin Plantinga, *God and Other Minds: A Study of the Rational Justification of Belief in God* (Ithaca, NY: Cornell University Press, 1967); *The Nature of Necessity* (Oxford, UK: Clarendon Press, 1974); *Warrant and Proper Function* (New York: Oxford University Press, 1993); *Warrant: The Current Debate* (Oxford, UK: Oxford University Press, 1993); *Warranted Christian Belief* (New York: Oxford University Press, 2000); Richard Swinburne, *The Coherence of Theism* (Oxford: Clarendon Press, 1977); *The Existence of God* (Oxford, UK: Clarendon Press, 1979).

27. Plantinga, *God and Other Minds; The Nature of Necessity; Warrant and Proper Function; Warrant: The Current Debate;* and *Warranted Christian Belief.*

28. Armstrong, *The Great Transformation.*

29. Ibid. See also Ian G. Barbour, *Religion and Science: Historical and Contemporary Issues* (San Francisco: HarperSanFrancisco, 1997).

30. Alexander Smith McCall, *The Careful Use of Compliments* (New York: Pantheon Books, 2007), 82–84; italics in original. Of course everyday life abounds with nonfictional "lived" accounts of spirituality; see Charles Taylor, *A Secular Age.*

31. Alister McGrath and Joanna Collicutt McGrath, *The Dawkins Delusion* (Downers Grove, IL: IVP Books, 2007), 31; italics in original.

32. See George Lakoff, *The Political Mind: Why You Can't Understand 21st-Century American Politics with an 18th-Century Brain* (New York: Viking, 2008).

NOTES TO CHAPTER 9

1. Italics added.

2. Rush Limbaugh, *TIME* (May 7, 2007): 22.

3. Ann Coulter, *TIME* (March 19, 2007): 17.

4. Allissa Rubin, "Cleric Switches Tactics to Meet Changes in Iraq," *New York Times* (July 19, 2007): A1.

5. Robert Hobbs and Mark Lombardi, *Global Networks* (New York: Independent Curators International, 2003).

6. Apple Dictionary, Version 2.0.2, 2005–2007.

7. Morley Winograd and Michael Hais, *Millennial Makeover: MySpace, YouTube, and the Future of American Politics* (New Brunswick, NJ: Rutgers University Press, 2008).

8. Arthur Schlesinger Jr., *The Cycles of American History* (New York: Mariner Books, 1999).

9. Paul Krugman, *The Conscience of a Liberal* (New York: Norton, 2007).

ABOUT THE AUTHORS

IAN I. MITROFF has spent his career using interdisciplinary approaches to find successful solutions to complex issues. He is an emeritus professor of the University of Southern California (USC), where he taught for twenty-six years. While he was at USC, he was the Harold Quinton Distinguished Professor of Business Policy in the Marshall School of Business; he also held a joint appointment in the Department of Journalism in the Annenberg School for Communication at USC, where he taught crisis management and served as associate director of the USC Center for Strategic Public Relations. Currently he is professor at Alliant International University; adjunct professor in the School of Public Health at St. Louis University and in the School of Public Health, Tropical Medicine and Rehabilitation Sciences, at James Cook University in Townsville, Australia; and visiting professor at the Center for Catastrophic Risk Management at the University of California at Berkeley.

In addition to teaching, Mitroff is president of Comprehensive Crisis Management, a consulting firm that offers an integrated approach to Crisis Management. For more than twenty-four years he has been sought out as an analyst and consultant on human-induced crises, including major incidents such as the Tylenol poisonings,

Bhopal, Three Mile Island, 9 / 11, the scandal in the Catholic Church, Enron, the war in Iraq, and the tsunami in Southeast Asia.

Mitroff is also author of several well-received books, including *Crisis Leadership* (Wiley, 2003), and *Why Some Companies Emerge Stronger and Better from a Crisis* (AMACOM, 2005).

ABRAHAM SILVERS provides statistical consulting and support in the design, database management, and analysis of health studies and clinical trials. He has consulted for a number of national and international pharmaceutical and biotech companies to address their need to meet FDA technical requirements in the areas of drugs, biologics, and devices.

Previously, Silvers was associate professor of Mathematics at California State University, Los Angeles. He was a Special Fellow at Stanford Medical School and director of statistics for the Stanford Heart Disease Prevention Program. He has served at the Mayo Clinic as a consultant and as director of statistical and epidemiological research for the Comprehensive Cancer Center. At Baylor College he was associate professor of medicine and senior statistician at the only National Heart Research and Demonstration Center sponsored by the National Institutes of Health (NIH). He has also served as professor of statistics at the University of Texas School of Public Health and at the University of California, San Francisco, where he developed and directed the Biostatistics Cancer Clinical Trial Group of the Cancer Center.

Silvers led an NIH team in developing an expert system for statistics as part of a computer resource for molecular biology research called Prophet. In addition, he has been an advisor for many institutes of NIH, for the World Health Organization, and for the Environmental Protection Agency.

Author of more than a hundred papers and book chapters, Silvers was elected a Fellow of the American Statistical Association (ASA) in 1988 for his contributions to clinical trial methodology. In 1993 he received the distinguished medal in statistics from the ASA.